First published 2014

Amberley Publishing
The Hill, Stroud
Gloucestershire, GL5 4EP

www.amberley-books.com

Copyright © W. B. Bartlett, 2014

British Library Cataloguing in Publication Data.
A catalogue record for this book is available from the British Library.

ISBN 978 1 4456 4367 0 (paperback)
ISBN 978 1 4456 4400 4 (ebook)

Typeset in 9.75pt on 12pt Minion Pro.
Typesetting and Origination by Amberley Publishing.

Printed in the UK.

Introduction

Britain and the British people were, in 1943, in much need of a boost. It was true of course that much had changed since the darkest days of 1940. The heroic triumph of the RAF in the Battle of Britain had helped remove the imminent threat of invasion and by now the country also had two great powers as her allies, because the German leadership had decided to launch unprovoked attacks on the Soviet Union as well as declaring war on the United States of America in the aftermath of the Japanese attack on Pearl Harbor.

It was also true that a great victory had been won by the British Army at El Alamein in November 1942, a triumph that famously caused the British Prime Minister Winston Churchill to remark that 'this is not the end. It is not even the beginning of the end, but it is, perhaps, the end of the beginning.' But, although church bells had been rung in recognition of the defeat of Rommel in the Egyptian desert, it would only look like a fork in the road to victory with the benefit of hindsight.

The clue was in the 'perhaps' in the Prime Minister's famous phrase, for Churchill would only remark later on that El Alamein was a definitive turning point for the British people, after which 'we never had a defeat'. For Britain, a long, hard slog still lay ahead. Between the beginning of 1942 and March 1943 a potentially crippling 7 million tons of British shipping had been lost to enemy action, mainly through U boat activity. On several occasions during this period, over a hundred ships had been lost in a month. Rationing continued to bite, strengthening the entirely accurate perception that this was an age of real and grim austerity. Neither was the news from abroad universally good; 16 May 1943, the very day of the raids, marked the formal conclusion to the brutal suppression by the Third Reich of the rebels in the Warsaw Ghetto, an act that sentenced thousands of Jews to death.

Luftwaffe activity had nevertheless sharply reduced since the Battle of Britain, though occasionally attacks would be launched which would create significant damage, most famously the so-called Baedeker raids (named after the famous tourist guides) launched in 1942 against a number of culturally significant cities: Bath, Exeter, Norwich, York and Canterbury. These raids came about in response to vastly increased RAF activity over Germany which had led in that same year to the first '1,000 bomber' raids against the enemy.

Despite the massive upsurge in the intensity of British air raids against Germany in 1942, Bomber Command still needed a major victory to convince its critics that it was headed in the right direction. Bomber Command's formidable Commander-in-Chief, Sir Arthur 'Bomber' Harris, had adopted a strategy known as 'area bombing'. This argued that the best approach was to attack key targets such as factories, towns and cities with heavy and, if necessary repeated, raids. However, there were many critics who did not agree with the strategy. A fierce argument had raged in the British High Command about how to best use the RAF during 1942 and, although Harris had won it in the short term, he needed a convincing victory to boost his standing and that of his Command. Only then would he feel secure in the knowledge that his Command enjoyed the confidence of the British leadership.

He would get such a victory on the night of 16/17 May 1943. At 0730 on the morning of the 17th, Squadron Leader Gerry Fray of 542 Squadron left RAF Benson in his Spitfire to fly towards the Ruhr to assess the impact of raids carried out there a few hours before. When he was about 150 miles from the Möhne dam (which was some 25 miles east of Dortmund), he could see industrial haze over the Ruhr area.

> On flying closer I saw what had seemed to be cloud was the sun shining on the floodwaters. I was flying at 30,000 feet and I looked down into the valley, which had seemed so peaceful three days before, but now it was a wide torrent with the sun shining on it.

He could in fact see an inland sea where there was none marked on the map. Fray was well placed to comment; he was the last British pilot to see the dam before it was breached on a reconnaissance flight on 15 May, and now he was the first to see it afterwards. He had flown the same reconnaissance missions frequently over several months and had got to know the area well. Now he could barely recognise it.

Shortly after this mission confirmed the success of the activities of the previous night, the news of a great victory was broken to the British people. Whilst the delivery may have been dry, the broadcast hinted at the fact that something extraordinary had taken place:

> This is London. The Air Ministry has just issued the following communiqué. In the early hours of this morning, a force of Lancasters of Bomber Command led by Wing Cdr G. P. Gibson DSO DFC attacked with mines the dams of the Möhne and Sorpe reservoirs. These control over two-thirds of the water storage capacity of the Ruhr basin. Reconnaissance later established that the Möhne dam had been breached over a length of one hundred yards, and that the power station below had been swept away. The Eder dam, which controls the headwaters of the Weser and Fulde valleys and operates several power stations, was also attacked and reported as breached. Photographs show the river below the dam in full flood. The attacks were pressed home from a very low level with great determination and coolness in the face of fierce resistance. Eight of the Lancasters are missing.

Churchill followed this up with a message that asked that the following greeting should be passed on:

> Please convey to the crew of the Lancasters of Number 617 Squadron who attacked the Möhne, Eder and Sorpe Dams my admiration and my congratulations on this outstanding and very gallant action. They have struck a blow that will have far-reaching effects.

It is highly unlikely that most people in Britain had any idea where the Möhne, Eder and Sorpe dams actually were. Even if they did, because of wartime censorship they would not know for years to come the full story of the extraordinary nature of the attack that had taken place. So secret were some of the details that when a major movie was made about the raids in 1955, some crucial details were incorrect. This included the shape of the bomb, which was still a classified secret. This was somewhat ironic as the Germans had a live working example in their possession on the morning after the raid.

There was of course much euphoria in Britain in the wake of this victory. Harris was ecstatic; this too was ironic as for some time he had been one of the biggest potential obstacles to the raids ever being launched at all. Churchill's delight was not just because of the impact on morale or the practical effects on German war production. Britain was in an increasingly problematic strategic situation. The Soviet Union, in the shape of its fierce leader Josef Stalin, was scathing about the lack of a meaningful 'second front' in Europe to distract the German armies from the bitter war that was still being fought in the East. Britain's main role as far as he was concerned was as a source of supply through its Arctic convoys. The British Empire, he felt, was otherwise increasingly an irrelevance in the modern world.

The daily meeting of the War Cabinet on 18 March 1943 offered up a case in point. Premier Stalin had sent two telegrams to Churchill. The first of them (both were sent on the 15th) was in response to a telegram from the Prime Minister which appeared to postpone any attempt to launch a 'second front'. In reply, the Soviet leader had noted that the 'uncertainty' of Churchill's comments aroused 'grave anxiety'. The second telegram was much more placatory, congratulating the British on the 'successful bombing' of Essen and other German cities. Clearly Bomber Command's efforts were not going completely unnoticed, even on the international scene.[4] Such positive news was welcome, especially as Britain was on the verge of postponing the North Atlantic convoys to the Soviet Union because of heavy German warship concentrations in the region. Anything that might help placate the formidable 'Uncle Joe' was to be welcomed.

Stalin's more dismissive views were shared by many in the US. There was frequent debate about whether the British were a 'busted flush' or not. Few Americans doubted the bravery of the British people but the record of the British Army in the early years of the war had been far from positive: Dunkirk may have been a gallant action but it was, when all was said and done, a retreat from the continent of Europe. An attempt to re-announce a return, albeit in a small-scale operation, in a raid on Dieppe in August 1942, was an unmitigated disaster with 60 per cent casualties and no significant objectives achieved.

Now Churchill had the victory he wanted in order to restore British pride and, more importantly, credibility. In contrast, *der Führer*, Adolf Hitler, had a headache. In the early hours of the 17th, his Armaments Minister, Albert Speer, had been woken by the news of an incredibly audacious attack. Shortly after, he had set off for the town of Werl – a few miles to the north of the Möhne valley and protected from the flood by a belt of higher land in between – in a Fieseler Storch light aircraft. As he approached the area, he could barely believe his eyes.

Speer witnessed the aftermath of one of the most incredible acts of daring of the entire war. The details when he started to establish them seemed unbelievable, but in this case fact was almost as strange as fiction. Most pertinently of all, had it not been for the genius and perseverance of an engineer and the bravery and skill of an RAF wing commander and his squadron, not to mention the talent of an often overlooked aircraft designer, the raid would never have happened in the first place.

The raids soon entered the realms of legend. Some details would appear in the press within a few days of the mission, though key facts would be suppressed in the interests of security. A decade later, the film would further add to the status of the raids in popular consciousness. Although not a complete distortion of the truth, rough edges were smoothed off, partly for the sake of artistic continuity perhaps but misleading nevertheless (Gibson's rather acerbic personality, for instance, was significantly played down in the movie). Attacks on two dams were shown but there were in fact four targets bombed (two unsuccessfully, hence their omission from the storyline). Other facts were plain wrong; Gibson is shown as having a flash of inspiration regarding how to work out the height at which his plane was flying while he's watching a West End show in London; in fact, it was from the rather more mundane source of an engineer's brain that the inspiration came.

And of course history is written by the victors, and this influenced the presentation of the film too. Nothing is said of the impact on human life of the chaos unleashed when the dams were burst. At the time, the loss of civilian life was larger than in any other raid. A large number of the dead were not even Germans but slave labourers in a camp in the path of the floods. This does not make for good material in a film perhaps, but it is as much a part of the true story as Gibson and his pet dog, 'Nigger', or the heroic (and very real) sacrifice of the British aircrews.

This is not meant as a carping criticism. Rather it is said to emphasise that there is little that is black or white in history; instead a rather large helping of grey is normally thrown in. Neither is it to moralise; the key lesson learned from wars is perhaps that people ought to be rather more careful about starting them because when they do it is not only the 'enemy' and his civilians that suffer but also one's own people too. The comments serve to make the point though that the raids were a source of great pain, both to the aircrews who suffered very heavy losses and to the civilians caught up in the effects.

A visit nowadays to the region where the raids took place, known as the 'Sauerland', holds rather pleasant surprises for the uninformed visitor. It is an area of great natural beauty (60 per cent of the area is currently part of a national park), and with the gently flowing Möhne river below the great dam it is a region of peace and tranquillity. With rolling hills around the stream (in a number of places it seems barely big enough to be called a river) rather than rugged mountains, it might easily remind a British visitor of the Wye valley. Some miles to the east, the Eder valley (in which the water flows in a different direction to that of the Möhne) is steeper and rockier, but the hills are still shrouded in pine trees and again it is a place of beauty. It is hard to imagine that these placid streams were turned into raging torrents as a result of what took place during the raids.

This book began as a tribute to the brave crews who took part in the raids. It ended, without diminishing the achievements of the courage and skill of the aircrews one jot, also as a journey into a place of beauty and tranquillity turned into one of terror and heartache. The paradox could not be more exquisitely painful, for war too takes some of the finest of human emotions – dedication, loyalty, devotion – to the point of death itself, and distorts them into a warped and deviant reflection of terrifying intensity. More than anything, at the end of my journey, the message was one of the futility and brutality of war and how, in the end, there are no real winners and losers but those who are left alive (often haunted by memories of terrible scenes witnessed or loved ones lost) and those who are not.

I have relied as much as I am able on the words of those who took part in the raids, as well as those on the receiving end, in the account that follows. Some, like Gibson, wrote their own books; many others were interviewed and their words then published. I have also trawled through the official records in an attempt to piece everything together and give a convincing narrative of these extraordinary raids. Only where there is evidence that contradicts some of the accounts have I introduced it. I do not do this lightly, nor do I insinuate any deliberate deception on the part of those whose detailed versions may sometimes be questioned. It is just that so much happened in such a short time that it is very easy to become confused by it all.

The events of that fateful night were telescoped into a few short hours. Between the time that the first plane took off at about 2130 on the evening of 16 May 1943 to the moment that the last surviving aircraft landed eight hours later, what was in fact a series of air raids was launched unlike any that had ever been seen before, or for that matter have ever been seen since. Now that the memories are receding, the story of sacrifice, suffering, bravery and resilience (not all of it from the British aircrews) deserves another telling if only as a reminder of the horror and tragedy of war and the very real dangers of complacency after decades of peace. There was plenty that was heroic and self-sacrificing in the raids and much to admire from that perspective, but in truth very little glory. We forget that particular lesson at our peril.

Wayne Bartlett
Bournemouth
16 May 2011

1

Last Minute Preparations at Scampton

Sunday 16 May 1943, up to 21.00 hours

With confirmation from Washington now in, the scene was set for the historic raids to take place. An important piece of last-minute information to arrive was reconnaissance from the dams that would be the targets. This confirmed that the water in the reservoirs was within a few feet of the top and only the Möhne appeared to be lightly defended. This was reassuring from several perspectives, as it suggested that there had been no leaks of information that had alerted the Germans to the imminent attack, and that the attackers would only have token resistance to deal with – and at only one dam. However, in the event, the resistance would be far fiercer at the Möhne dam than suspected and the very terrain over which the planes would have to approach the target would act as a defence mechanism for the dams.

For one man in particular, Flight Engineer John Pulford, who was flying with Gibson, this was a particularly poignant time. His father had just died and he had been given compassionate leave to attend the funeral. Just in case, he was accompanied by military policemen who were there to ensure that he did not let any sensitive information slip (Gibson did not like Pulford particularly and thought him 'dull' and this may have added to his sensitivity about the issue). What was already a traumatic personal experience was made considerably worse by the close watch that he was kept under, but no chances could be taken.

The orders for the raid, still classified 'top secret' to all but a privileged few, were to be found in No. 5 Group Operation Order No. B.976. They noted that 'destruction of Target X [the Möhne dam] alone would bring about a serious shortage of water for drinking purposes and industrial supplies'. Target Z, the Sorpe dam, was to be the next priority – that being the case, it is not clear why the Eder was a secondary target for Gibson's flight rather than this. It was said that the destruction of Target Y, the Eder dam, would 'seriously hamper transport in the Mittelland canal and in the Weser, and would probably lead to almost complete cessation of the great volume of traffic now using these waterways'. However, that would prove to be a much smaller result than would be the case if the Sorpe were successfully attacked.

Due to the fact that the dams would be at their maximum capacity at this time, which would result in the greatest potential for damage should their walls be breached, the raids should be launched on the first suitable date after 15 May 1943. This turned out to be Sunday 16 May. Twenty Lancasters should take part. (Although in the event, due to illness among some of the crews, only nineteen would actually fly. These illnesses were actually somewhat fortuitous as there were only nineteen suitably adapted bombers fit to fly on the raid.)

It was deemed likely that three effective attacks might be needed to breach the Möhne dam but in any event the attacks should continue until this had been done. The wave of aircraft attacking this dam should then, once this objective had been achieved, move on to the Eder dam. If this too should be breached by the aircraft designated as part of this first wave, then they should move on to the Sorpe dam.

The second wave, which was to cross the coast of the Continent at the same time as the first (but further north), was to attack the Sorpe while the third wave, which was to follow the same route as the first (but would leave later), was to effectively be an airborne reserve that could be recalled should all objectives have been achieved by the first two waves.

There would be a two-and-a-half-hour gap between the first wave and the third. In the event, the uses to which the reserve was put was one of the least successful elements of the mission as it was deployed so piecemeal that it could not make a real impact and was inadequately briefed on some of the targets it was given. It also suffered significant losses from enemy defences that were much more aware of what was going on over Germany by the time that their wave set out.

The aircraft were not to fly above 1,500 feet when they were in English airspace. On crossing the English coastline they were to descend to a height of 60 feet throughout the rest of their journey to their targets and for most of their trip back again. On reaching a point 10 miles away from the targets, the leader of each wave was to ascend to a height of 1,000 feet. At this point, VHF radio contact should be made by each pilot with the leader. For the first wave the bomb, described as 'the special store', should be set to spin from 10 minutes before the time that any attack was launched. However, for the attack on the Sorpe dam the bomb was not to be spun at all as it was not required to skim across the surface but would be dropped at right angles to the target.

The leader of the first wave, who was of course to be Gibson, was to launch the first attack on the Möhne dam and then direct all others there and then on to the Eder once he was satisfied that the raid on the first target had been a success. Even if the Möhne dam were damaged, Gibson could carry on attacking it to widen the breach made provided that there were at least three aircraft left to proceed to the Eder dam (again, something of an anomaly given its relative unimportance).

For all attacks there should be a gap of at least 3 minutes between each bomb drop – this would give time for both any damage to be assessed and also for any turbulence in the water to die down to make the path of the next bomb unleashed truer. The pilot of each plane was to be responsible for the line of attack, the navigator for its height, the bomb-aimer for the range and the flight engineer for the speed. On Targets X and Y a Very pistol was to be fired from the aircraft when they were immediately over the target dam. For Target Z the Very pistol cartridge was to be fired as each bomb was dropped. All watches should be synchronised to BBC time before take-off.

A change was also to be made to the guns to be used in the planes. Normally there would be tracer included at a rate of every two or three bullets but now all of them were to be Mk VI night tracer rounds. The thinking behind this was that it would 'look more fearsome to the Germans' and anything that could be done to put off the flak gunners at the Möhne was to be welcomed. The white light might also confuse the Germans into thinking that cannon shells were being fired.

The day began early for Gibson who had spent an uncomfortable night. As well as the anxiety he felt about the now imminent mission and the distress at the tragic loss of Nigger, Gibson's feet were also playing up. He was up and about at 0530 and made his way to the surgery. Dr Upton, who treated him, was unable to do much for him as he was made aware that Gibson would be flying later that day, which meant that pain-killers were out of the question. Gibson would just have to grin and bear it.

During the course of Sunday 16 May, it would become increasingly obvious around the base that a major raid was likely to be launched within hours. At just after 0900 Gibson hinted to Humphries in his office that there was to be a major action that day. However, Humphries was not to let anyone else know even this until further orders were given. Gibson told him that he would apprise him of details of mealtimes and a night-flying programme later that day, then disappeared carrying a bulky red file marked 'Most Secret'. The game was most definitely afoot.

Even now attention was being devoted to how the news of the raids should be regulated so that ultimate secrecy could be maintained not only before the mission but also after it. Press access to Group staff or aircrew was to be strictly regulated. All press communiqués were to be 'strictly controlled and supervised' by the Air Ministry. Only very limited information was to be released which would tell very little to anybody; tying in with a plan developed at a meeting at King Charles Street on 25 March 1943, it was to be emphasised in any communiqué issued after the raids that 'in the event, the crews displayed the greatest skill in executing the operation as planned'.

Later on, Humphries received from Gibson firm details of the times that the night-flying programme for the day was to begin and end. There was much for Humphries now to prepare. Buses needed to be organised to take the aircrews out to their planes and meals needed to be synchronised with the flight times. Flying rations needed to be made available, including coffee and refreshments that the crews could carry with them. It was also Humphries's job to accept cash, wills and letters for next of kin from anyone who was due to fly.

Humphries's major problem was a surprisingly mundane one. He asked the WAAF sergeant in charge of the mess kitchen for a special meal but she stubbornly refused to comply, saying that she had no specific orders to do so. Humphries was left with virtually no option but to tell her that this was not a normal training flight today but that the men were going into action. Informed of this, her attitude changed at once and she confirmed that the meals requested would indeed be prepared.

Despite the building sense of excitement, even now secrecy was rigorously maintained by those in the know. It was perhaps a surprise that the element of secrecy was so well maintained during the build-up to the raids. Scampton was shared with another unit, 57 Squadron, but there was barely a hint of anything unusual afoot coming from 617 Squadron at any point. The members of the newly formed unit had performed their part in maintaining secrecy very well indeed. The greater concerns, as has been seen, came from sources outside the squadron.

The ground crews would also be frantically busy with last-minute preparations to attend to. This was the period at which they really came into their own. One oversight on their part could have disastrous consequences. One of their main tasks was to test the compasses with and without the weapon in place as the huge mass of metal had a major effect on their accuracy. Deviations were then noted and placed in the plane for future reference. Without this information a pilot could be miles off course and completely lost – this would be a problem especially for Joe McCarthy later that day.

Then of course the bombs needed to be fitted and balanced; no easy task with a weight of nearly 10,000 lb involved. The planes would also carry six 4-lb 'stick' incendiary devices and these would also prove to be of use to some of the crews during the raid. In addition, the planes needed to be fuelled up: 1,740 gallons each for the long journey to their targets and back (though the distance involved was well within the Lancasters' range of 850 miles). This was a moment of intensive activity, with so much to be done and a strict deadline within which to complete their tasks. There would be no rest until the planes were safely up and away and even then only a few hours of snatched sleep would be possible before the planes returned again.

It could also be a dangerous period. There was a moment of panic while the bombs were being loaded. The one being fitted to Martin's plane dropped out onto the tarmac. Bomb-aimer Bob Hay yelled that it might have fused itself and could explode within a minute.

Everyone frantically exited the Lancaster as quickly as they could. Martin rushed off to pick up the Armaments Officer, 'Doc' Watson, who, with breath-taking calmness, inspected the weapon and told everybody not to panic as the bomb had not fused after all.

This was no idle panic though as memories of a recent serious incident at Scampton were still fresh. On 15 March 1943, a bomb was accidentally released from a 57 Squadron Lancaster. The weapon subsequently detonated and destroyed this plane and four visiting 50 Squadron aircraft parked nearby. This would have a catastrophic impact on the raid should any similar incident occur given the fact that all the planes had been specially modified. With no spares at hand, the raids might not have happened at all.

The secret of the raids would gradually and selectively be disclosed during the course of the day. It was late morning when the first briefings were held; there would be several over the course of the day. There would be a progressive rolling out of information as the day went on. At midday, the SASO, Group Captain Satterly, passed on the orders to Wing Commander Dunn, 5 Group's Chief Signals Officer, so that signals could be put in place for the raid. Satterly was responsible for the detailed plans for the raid but is often overlooked in histories of the raid. The plan would not be perfect but it would achieve a number of its objectives, so some credit should go to Satterly for that.

In these first briefings, Gibson and Wallis briefed the pilots and navigators while Wing Commander Dunn, 5 Group's Chief Signals Officer, briefed the wireless operators. The plans of attack were explained. Gibson would be in first from the first wave of nine planes to the Möhne and, if that was successfully breached, then on to the Eder. New Yorker Joe McCarthy would lead a wave of five planes to the Sorpe. Flight Sergeant Townsend would be in charge of six planes as a flexible reserve (there would only be five in the event due to illness and a lack of planes). After lunch at 1400, the bomb-aimers and gunners joined the navigators and pilots. More and more people were now starting to learn of the raids and their targets, though there were still stringent measures being taken to ensure that the news did not leak outside the base.

Initial briefings on radio control and the route to be taken – some 400 miles of it – were held. Those who had this briefing were still sworn to secrecy as far as the other crew members were concerned. At these initial meetings, contour scale models of the Möhne and

Sorpe dams were unveiled. There was though no model of the Eder to study; it would not arrive until after the raids were all over. Bomb-aimer Leonard Sumpter later remarked that 'the first time I saw the Eder was when I got there'.

It was a boiling hot day, unusually so for the time of year, and there was frantic activity with ground crews buzzing around now getting everything ready for the mission. Slow-moving tractors trundled around the airfield laden with bombs to be loaded onto the planes. Summers and Wallis walked around the planes ensuring as far as they were able that everything was right. The crews spent three hours of the afternoon studying maps of where they were headed. The last-minute briefings had helped to preserve the element of surprise.

But the downside of this was that the crews had little time to become familiar with the route and the targets. In retrospect this would create significant problems. A number of crews flew off course and some of them would pay the ultimate price for this error. Others would find it difficult to locate the right targets; for the reserve wave in particular, effectiveness would be significantly compromised by the lack of clear instructions for where they should head. This would compromise the achievement of some of the raid's objectives.

There were also some last-minute problems to be dealt with. Wallis noticed that the wrong oil was being used for some of the equipment and alternative supplies had to be found with some difficulty. There was also a shortage of spare planes. With one plane out of commission there were no spares and it was important to rectify this just in case of a last-minute hitch. In addition to the 464 Lancasters delivered to Scampton, three other planes had been developed and delivered elsewhere for use in ongoing testing.

One of them was at Boscombe Down in Wiltshire. Commander H. C. Bergel was delegated to fly it up to Scampton as a reserve (this would turn out to be a particularly useful move as it happened). He arrived, accompanied by Third Officer Salter of the Air Transport Auxiliary, with what would be designated plane AJ-T at 1530. There was no time to mount the TR1143 radio or the spotlights to the aircraft. This could have been disastrous if the plane needed to be used in an attack on the dams at the Möhne or Eder, though as it happened this would not be the case, which was just as well. Another plane was also flown in but this was so last-minute that it arrived too late to be of any use. After the raids, it would be given the code AJ-C, replacing a plane piloted by Pilot Officer Warner Ottley which would no longer exist by the time that the raids were over.

These last-minute arrivals were something of an oversight in the plan. It would have been much more sensible to deliver them before this late hour, especially as two planes had been damaged in the recent training flights. The design of the aircraft also came as a surprise to those pilots who were required to fly them up to Scampton (who were not their test pilots). When flying his plane, Bergel wondered why the bomb-bay was so different and had no idea what some of the equipment on the instrument panel referred to. He was even more surprised when he arrived at Scampton to see other aircraft in the same condition, one with a slowly rotating object in its belly.

Bergel's curiosity was roused but he was warned off before he could ask too many questions – the suggestion that those involved with the project had been confined to base for the last eleven weeks did the trick as it implied that the same thing might happen to him if he became too inquisitive. Bergel boarded a waiting Anson and flew back to his home base, unaware at the time of the small part he was playing in creating history.

At 1610 a 'secret cypher message' was sent from 5 Group HQ to the Officer Commanding at Scampton (Whitworth). Its message was simplicity itself but gave the green light for one of the most amazing air raids ever launched. It simply said, 'Executive operation Chastise 16/5/43 zero hours'. The raids were on.

ll crews of 617 Squadron were directed to assemble for a report in the briefing room at 1800. Over 130 young men crowded in, waiting to hear the final details of what they had been training for so hard for the past couple of months. Wallis would play a key role in the discussions, explaining key facts and figures about the dams and how difficult they would be to crack.

This was a general briefing for all crew members. There were 132 of these in the room along with Gibson, senior officers and Wallis sitting on a dais at the front of the room. There was also a civilian, Herbert Jeffree, who was a scientist who worked with Wallis and, in a potentially serious breach of security, had bluffed his way into the room; despite the tight controls over the operation, there was a gatecrasher at the briefing. The room was packed with the luminaries lined up at the front of the briefing room where there was a large map of Germany on the wall, covered over for the time being with a black curtain. It was time to begin the briefing.

Gibson opened proceedings and told the crews that the target was to be the great dams of Germany. He then introduced Wallis, who relayed more about the problems he had had with developing the weapons and put on a brave face but privately he was worried. Reality was starting to hit home as he earlier told Gibson, 'You know, I hardly look upon this as an operational mission. My job has just been to develop something which will break down a dam wall. I look upon this raid as my last great experiment to see if it can be done on the actual thing.' He also said to Gibson, 'I hope they all come back.' The scientist was starting to understand the potential human cost involved.

It was 'early in 1942' according to his own recollection that Wallis had the idea of a ricocheting bomb to breach the dams (though as noted already the idea of a 'hydroplane skimmer' device had already been thought of). His daughter, Mary Stopes Roe, was later reminded of holidays in the Isle of Purbeck in Dorset when they would skim stones across the surface of the sea. He would later famously experiment with his children's marbles before developing spherical devices at Vickers to prove that a bomb could be developed. He wrote up his ideas in a paper called 'Spherical Bomb – Surface Torpedo'.

There was though something of the archetypal British eccentricity in his early experiments; when he catapulted wooden spheres across Silvermere Lake at Byfleet, they were recovered from the water by his formidable secretary, Amy Gentry, who would row out in a rowing boat to pick them up. Despite what could be his very dominant personality, she did not hesitate to berate him when he occasionally stood up in the boat during an overexcited reaction and threaten to sink it.

Wallis approached Professor P. M. S. Blackett, Scientific Adviser to the Admiralty, with his ideas about the 'bouncing bomb' as he considered the weapon would be well suited to the Fleet Air Arm, but Blackett also saw its uses for the RAF and forwarded it to Tizard, who visited Wallis shortly afterwards. They got on well. Within days, Wallis had moved his testing to the rather more formal surroundings of the ship-testing tank at the National Physical Laboratory (NPL) at Teddington.

Here it was proved that spinning the prototype bomb before release would make it more effective. The idea of using backspin rather than topspin came from a Vickers aircraft engineer, George Edwards, who as a cricketer felt that it would be more appropriate. Forward spin would tend to sink the bomb before it reached the target, whereas back spin would encourage it to be propelled until it hit the dam wall and rolled down it before exploding, thus making it much more effective.

Despite his worries about the human cost, Wallis was still a scientist at heart. He concluded his remarks to his assembled audience with the following comments: 'You gentlemen are really carrying out the third of three experiments. We have tried it out on model dams, also a dam one-fifth of the size of the Möhne dam. I cannot guarantee it will come off but I hope it will.' When he sat down, he muttered that 'they must have thought it was Father Christmas talking to them'. Wallis's reactions after he heard of the heavy losses later suffered in the raids give all the evidence of a man completely in shock at their scale. Judging by his comments before the mission, the high number of casualties was something that he was not expecting except for the odd pessimistic moment when the true dangers of the raids broke in.

Wallis in his briefing advised that the planes should fly at a speed of 220 mph and at a height of 60 feet. The bomb should be dropped 410 yards from the dam wall and should then bounce three times before hitting it, rolling down to a depth of 30 feet and then exploding. Reconnaissance had been taking place for two months to monitor the rising of the water levels and the weather forecast was good for that evening. It was the right time to go.

Wallis was very enthusiastic in his presentation and drew models on the blackboard rather than using slides. He came across as a kindly man, very clever and something of a father figure. He also inspired confidence despite the novel nature of the mission. But Sergeant Jim Clay, a bomb-aimer with Les Munro, thought that 'it seemed incongruous that this kindly and quietly spoken man, Barnes Wallis, should be involved with devastation'.

Cochrane was another of those who spoke to the men and told the crews that the raids might do a lot of damage but 'it may be a secret until after the war. So don't think you are going to get your pictures in the papers.' In the event, he could not have been more wrong. But at this point in proceedings the crews were reminded that they must keep every detail of the raid secret, even when they returned to England. There were other uses for the weapon, they were told, with the naval weapon codenamed Highball in mind.

Cochrane's speech was followed by more words from Gibson, who repeated the details of the roles of the three waves to all the crew.

Ever a stickler for detail, he took no chance that anybody in the room was unsure of their role in the historic mission that lay before them. There was a discussion following this during which the interloper Jeffree, showing considerable brass neck, pointed out that it might be dangerous to return to base with an undropped bomb that was still fused. Gibson told the crews that no one was to bring an unused bomb back, an injunction that not everyone would comply with.

Given the fact that they were relatively lightly defended, there was widespread relief that the dams were the target. There had been some speculation about what the target might be; the most popular choice was the U-boat pens on the Atlantic coast which were heavily defended. Others thought, as in Gibson's original reaction, that it was the *Tirpitz*. But most were fatalistic about coming back anyway, though some did not take any special precautions – Navigator Arthur Hobday, for example, did not take the precaution of making a will, perhaps thinking that he would be tempting fate by doing so.

Although some of those present had already had one earlier briefing on the raid – or perhaps because of the fact, as they knew, that it would call for precision flying of the highest order – the atmosphere in the briefing room was very tense. Sergeant Frederick Sutherland thought it was like going into an exam room. He did not like what he heard, telling himself that 'this was going to be really touch and go'. However, some tried to reassure themselves by focusing on certain aspects of the briefing; Hobday told himself, for example, that navigation would be helped by canals which were quite visible at night. Navigator Dudley Heal said that many of the men went to the bar and had a drink, shaking their heads at attacking the dams at a height of 60 feet. This would suggest that in some quarters normal injunctions against drinking on the eve of a raid went out of the window.

While the briefings were taking place, Humphries returned to his room. He had noticed a lot of strange faces around the place belonging to people that he did not recognise, including that of Wallis. Despite his closeness to Gibson, Humphries still had no idea where the raids were headed. But he knew that whatever was happening was big.

As the crews left the briefing room there was much to be done before their departure and not a lot of time to do it. There were mundane details to be attended to, such as a meal in the mess. Then there were operational matters to consider. Navigators had to make sure that their routes were properly prepared. Notes were marked on the route and power lines were marked with red crayon: the pylons were 100 feet high in the Netherlands but the cables between them sagged dangerously lower, forming a deathly spider's web for any aircraft that was flying too close to them. The crew went back to their rooms for a wash or a bath or a shave – anything that might bring a modicum of normality and relaxation when they were faced with their epic task.

Flight rations also needed to be issued to the crews: some bars of chocolate, tins of orange juice, an orange, chewing gum, Horlicks tablets. Escape equipment also had to be handed out: a wallet with the currency of the countries that the crew were flying over, a compass, morphine with needles. There was also a silk map issued which covered the countries that were en route. There was always a chance, however slim, of an escape should a plane be brought down over enemy territory, and one of the crew would certainly give the Germans a run for their money before the night was out.

Attention to secrecy was still all important. Ruth Ive, a WAAF who was a radio operator, was called into the telephone exchange to make sure that no one was breaching the rule that there should be no external phone calls by eavesdropping on all attempted conversations; she was to disconnect anyone who was trying to break the injunction. However, she herself had no idea that the raid was on.

At 1930 the crews went off to their meal of egg and bacon with an extra egg for anyone who was flying that night. Weak jokes were made about who would have the spare egg of crew members who did not return, a typical piece of black humour that helped to defuse the tension. There was no time to hang about with the meal; there was just an hour until the crews had to make their way out to their aircraft.

Time took on its own momentum now, although its pace varied from man to man. To some it flew past; to others it dragged interminably. Harry Humphries later remarked that the scenes outside the crew rooms were unforgettable. Some crews had 'don't give a damn' looks on their faces while others looked grim and determined.

Even the ground crew felt a sense of emotional involvement. Some of them had been allocated to one aircraft, so they had sometimes formed a strong relationship with the crews, though it varied depending on the personality and approach of the pilot. Other ground crew were responsible for covering a number of aircraft but even then it was possible to have a special affinity for one or more of them – Beck Parsons of the ground crew, for example, thought very highly of Mick Martin. A number of ground crew had gone up with the planes when they were training, which helped to form an even closer bond.

The time for preparation was almost complete and the time for action was drawing close. As the hour for departure approached, Humphries was on hand to make sure that all the busses ordered to take the crews out to their planes had arrived as planned. Small details needed to be carefully choreographed as time was of the essence – the last thing needed was any delay as it might result in the bombers flying back from the raids in broad daylight. As the busses were loaded, pilot Dave Shannon was the last to get on, in return for which a number of sarcastic comments were pointed in his direction. The weather was warm and inviting, a pleasant, balmy evening in other circumstances, but few of the crew members would have much appreciated the tranquillity.

In the distance across the airfield the Lancasters stood silently and ominously, waiting to take off for a destination that was still unknown to most people other than the aircrews. Some of the latter were lying around on the ground, Mae Wests and parachutes scattered carelessly around them. Nineteen planes, 133 pilots and crewmen, not just British but also Canadians, Australians and New Zealanders (and, if one were to be pedantic, an American who had enlisted in the Royal Canadian Air Force). The cosmopolitan nature of the crews was in fact broadly representative of the nature of Bomber Command in 1943; in January of that year, 37 per cent of all the Command's pilots were Australians, New Zealanders or Canadians, a figure that would rise to 45 per cent later in the war.

Gibson arrived in his car. Getting out, he walked around the men chatting to them, putting minds at rest and offering an encouraging word or two to those who needed it. Humphries walked over to speak to him but before he could do so Flight Lieutenant Trevor-Roper, one of Gibson's crew, greeted him with a characteristically rude 'hello short arse'. Humphries did not take kindly to this but rather than further antagonise Trevor-Roper he just blushed. To his subsequent question to Gibson about whether anything was needed, the Wing Commander just asked that plenty of beer should be available for the party that they would be having when they came back. Gibson thought for a second and then added ominously, 'I hope'.

Some of the men carried mascots or good-luck charms. Martin

for example always carried a toy koala bear, while Gibson had a German Mae West inflatable lifejacket he had had since early in the war. Maltby always took an old, dirty hat with him. Gibson perhaps thought that he was in receipt of a lucky omen; his plane's code was AJ-G, his father's initials – and this was his father's birthday.

By 2030 the crews were out by their aircraft waiting to board. Moods varied; Hopgood's crew for example were mostly engaged in a game of cricket. Others though were more reserved. Hopgood's navigator, Flight Officer K. Earnshaw, predicted that eight aircraft would not come back, a figure that would be exactly right.

It was a sentiment shared by his pilot. Hopgood had confided to Dave Shannon when they shared a cigarette behind the hangar before taking off: 'I think this is going to be a tough one, and I don't think I'm coming back, Dave.' Wireless operator Abraham Garshowitz chalked a message on the bomb of his plane: 'never has so much been expected of so few' – a Churchillian sentiment that probably many of the men shared.

These planes would not be the only British aircraft flying that night. On the same evening there were actions by other British planes that might throw the German defences off their guard, but these were limited as the full moon made it a dangerous night for flying. Eight Mosquitoes were deputed to attack four German cities, and six German Luftwaffe bases in the Netherlands were also to receive unwelcome visits. Fifty-four planes were to drop mines in the German Bight while ten others were to drop leaflets in France. These activities might at least help to focus the German defences elsewhere while the raids were in progress.

Now the waiting was over and it was time to board the strangely-laden Lancasters. There was a strict order in which men boarded, based on where they were to be sitting in the plane. The bomb-aimer was first, scrambling up a small ladder and through the rear starboard door, from where he climbed forward into the nose. This was not easy; there was a high spar across the middle of the plane which made access from the rear to the forward areas difficult – this could be disastrous if the plane had to be abandoned quickly, especially if a man in front of the spar was injured and immobile.

Placed above the bomb-aimer in the forward part of the plane would be the front gunner, his feet in stirrups to stop him from getting in the way of the bomb-aimer, who was laid face downwards on the floor right at the front of the aircraft. Perched behind his .303

Browning machine guns, the front gunner would have a vital role to play against the flak gunners in the vicinity of the Möhne dam.

Then came the pilot, followed by his flight engineer. The latter would assist the pilot during take-off and landing and would keep an eye on the instruments while the aircraft was in flight. Judging from the small number of medals handed out after the raids, the flight engineer was considered a rather unsung hero, there only to help the pilot out, though in an emergency it would be his job to take over the controls if the pilot were killed or seriously injured.

Last of all came the navigator, the wireless operator and finally the rear gunner. Passing the chemical Elsan toilet on board, the rear gunner made his way into the rear turret. This position was precarious and also freezing cold. Worst of all, it was hard to get out of quickly. Just to compound the problem, there was not enough room in the turret to wear a parachute in it so getting out of a burning aircraft quickly would be very difficult for someone in this position.

The inside of the Lancaster left little room to manoeuvre. It was uncomfortable in other ways too. The temperature on board varied according to altitude and how good the engines were; it also depended on where you were sitting in it. The pilot, the engineer, the bomb-aimer and the navigator sat forward while the radio operator sat behind them, behind the massive main spar which everyone had to climb over to reach the front of the plane. The navigator sat at a table and could not see outside – only the bomb-aimer, the pilot and the engineer could. The navigator therefore relied on those who could see to feed him with landmarks from the ground that he could use to plot their position.

It was now time for the off, for the planes to climb cumbersomely into the sky, weighed down with their heavy burden and headed for their appointment with destiny. Gibson and his crew, along with the others, climbed the rickety-looking steps into their planes. Flying Officer Bellamy was on hand to snap a number of historic photos as they did so, Gibson thinking that 'these men certainly choose the queerest times'. In any event, he entered into the spirit of the occasion, looking back towards Bellamy and allegedly telling him, 'Make sure you send a copy back to my wife!'

There were only nine photographs in all taken of the moments before and after the raid at Scampton and only four of them were released to the public, meaning that for all the remarkable events that were about to unfold there was very little photographic record of the raids though plenty of their aftermath. A famous photograph of Gibson standing at the top of the rickety ladder into his plane at the head of his crew strikes a slightly artificial pose as it would not normally be the pilot who was first into the plane. Still, a hero needs to adopt a hero's posture and it was understandable photographic licence for this slightly staged arrangement to be employed.

The clock was now ticking towards zero hour and a great moment of truth was at hand. Wallis's bombs had worked well, if not consistently, in trials and the crews had become dab hands at low flying. But they had never yet experienced such low flying while being fired at by German guns. Now their trial by fire was about to begin. Some would pass with flying colours. Others would pay the ultimate price for failure.

2

Take-off & Flight Over the North Sea

21.00–22.50, Sunday 16 May

The nerves were now really starting to kick in. With the crews now boarded, it was just a question of waiting for the signal to take off, and the waiting could seem endless. Unlike most raids, which just formed part of a seemingly non-stop procession of sorties, men had been training specifically for this one. This was a special mission and they were by definition special aircrews but they all faced a special risk. The very uniqueness of what lay before them only served to set the nerves even more on edge.

If the three waves scheduled to take part in the raids, the designated first wave, led by Gibson, would, counter-intuitively, take off after the wave which was due to attack the Sorpe, led by Joe McCarthy. This was because the latter group of aircraft was flying by a northerly route and had further to go, even though the Sorpe and Möhne dams were within a few miles of each other.

It was at 2110 that Flight Lieutenant Hutchison in Gibson's plane gave the signal by Very light for the planes to start their engines. This was the instruction for all first and second wave planes to start up and move around the perimeter and begin preparations for take-off. In the planes that were due to begin their journey in the next twenty minutes or so, ignitions were started and starter buttons pressed. Most of the aircraft chugged and spluttered into life but in one of them at once a problem became apparent. Joe McCarthy's plane (code

AJ-Q) had a problem with a glycol (coolant) leak with the starboard outer engine which meant that it would not be going anywhere that night. The crew abandoned the plane as fast as they could and sought out a replacement.

This one event could have been disastrous. As the leader of the raid on the Sorpe, McCarthy had a particularly important role, though the logistics of the attack on the dam were different to those of the raid against the Möhne. McCarthy's should have been the first plane to take off but that was not going to happen. It was just as well that Commander Bergel had flown up a replacement that afternoon as there was no other plane available. It was also a stroke of luck that there were nineteen planes available and nineteen crews as two of those who were supposed to be involved were incapacitated.

This was because there was illness affecting two crews which consequently could not fly. Those involved were Pilot Officer Divall and Flight Lieutenant Wilson and their crews (the latter man should have flown on the mission against the Sorpe dam, which meant that this wave was already a plane down without McCarthy dropping out). Divall had a knee injury and Wilson was ill. But if their luck was in on this particular night, this was certainly not to continue in the future; their reprieve was temporary as both would be killed in September 1943 during a catastrophic raid on the Dortmund – Ems Canal. Divall had been due to fly with the reserve wave but it is not at all clear that a plane would have been available for him to fly anyway.

McCarthy came running back towards the hangars from his abandoned plane looking, according to Humphries, 'like a runaway tank'. Desperate to see the action, the thought must have crossed his mind that if another plane was out of action then someone might get there before him to bag the 'spare'. McCarthy originated from Brooklyn, a part of the world whose residents were not renowned for their patience. He was a big man and the sight of him this angry must have been extremely disconcerting. Flight Sergeant 'Chiefy' Powell, an unheralded backroom hero of the raids, did his best to calm him down.

This, however, was not easy, for the spare plane (which would be designated AJ-T) had not been fully prepared for the mission. It had not yet been equipped with a compass card, which was vital given the difficulties in navigating on the raid. McCarthy furiously demanded to know, 'Where are those lazy, idle, incompetent compass adjusters?' According to Humphries, 'Mac' was in something of a mess, his rage having disturbed his equanimity. Humphries suggested that he should calm down and everything should be alright.

This was not a good start. Not only would the wave attacking the Sorpe dam be without its leader when it took off but, if and when McCarthy did manage to get up, it would be difficult for him to be at his best given this unsettling start to his flight. That said, it was clear that McCarthy was spoiling for a fight and it would take quite exceptional adverse circumstances to dampen his martial spirit. But these problems with the leader of the Sorpe wave were an entirely appropriate portent for what was to follow as far as this particular wave was concerned.

At 2128, another signal was given showing that it was now time to take off. In the absence of McCarthy, it was Flight Lieutenant Robert Barlow who was first away. There was a little caravan at the edge of the runway instead of a control tower and from inside this a green Aldis light was to be shown when the moment for take-off had arrived. The planes lined up and the crews aboard waited with a mixture of apprehension and excitement. When at last the light shone forth, they roared down the grass runway, starting at its southern end. It was an extra long run as the weight of the planes was especially heavy. The pilots all knew that there was no pulling out at the last moment – once the planes were committed that was it.

The moment of take-off was therefore one of great tension. The Lancaster was a much heavier bomber than any of the men would have been used to at the start of the war; for example, it was about twice the aircraft, weight-wise, that the Wellington was. Take-off safety speed was 130 mph so the aircrew were always reliant on the four engines holding out while under extreme pressure during the build-up to take-off and during take-off itself. This was exacerbated because of the heavy load that the planes were carrying.

The Sorpe wave now led the way into battle minus, at this stage, its leader. The true purpose of the raid on the Sorpe was, according to Gibson in his later account of the raids, a diversionary one. He said that the reason for routeing them far to the north of the wave that was headed for the Möhne was to get them to draw off the night fighters. Then they were to fly down to the Sorpe and the attack there was to take the fighters again away from the planes attacking the Möhne.

Yet this explanation of the diversionary role of the planes attacking the Sorpe is not at all convincing. The official order for the raid gives no such suggestion. The Möhne dam is recognised as the most important target for sure, but the Sorpe was officially the next most important. To devastate the Ruhr valley to the extent desired, both would need to be breached. As supporting evidence that the Sorpe was never intended as a diversion, paragraph 27 of the order is devoted entirely to the issue of diversionary attacks but makes no mention of the attack on the Sorpe dam in this respect and merely refers to the other diversionary raids taking place across the Continent that night.

A more likely explanation is that Gibson later sought to play down the attacks on the Sorpe because they were the least successful part of the raid. This was through no fault of the pilots, some of whom lost their lives in the mission while others dropped their bombs after taking great care to follow instructions. The problem was that the weapon they were carrying was simply not up to the task of breaking the Sorpe dam open given its different construction. This would have been an embarrassing admission given the euphoria that attended the successes enjoyed by the raids and therefore it was much more convenient to suggest that the attack on the Sorpe was a diversion all along.

With Barlow in the lead, the wave headed for the Sorpe set off at one-minute intervals. At 2129, Flight Lieutenant Munro of the RNZAF in AJ-W took off, followed at 2130 by Pilot Officer Vernon Byers in AJ-K and then Pilot Officer Geoffrey Rice in AJ-H at 2131. These first four planes flew in a long formation at around 50 feet at a speed of 180 mph about 3 miles apart. They made their way towards the east, across the waters that would take them right into the heart of the enemy's lair.

As they made their way towards the North Sea on a northerly route that would take them over the Netherlands, the scene was now set for Gibson at the head of the first wave to set off for the Möhne. Whitworth, the Scampton base commander, made his way on board the plane to wish Gibson luck; Gibson smiled back with a weak grin. A photographer ran up and asked to take his photo: weird timing again, thought Gibson. Despite his implacable exterior, Gibson later admitted to being very nervous but now it was time to go. There is no reason to doubt that he really was anxious and the calm exterior probably reflected more a leader who did not wish to betray his fears rather than any lack of nerves.

Gibson's wave now prepared to roll off down the grass runways and into the air. At 2139 the green light from the Aldis lamp was given for his flight. Alongside him were 'Hoppy' Hopgood (in AJ-M) and 'Mick' Martin (in AJ-P). Unlike the Sorpe wave, they took off in a loose 'vic' formation (a 'vic' was a triangle of planes with one in the lead and two slightly back to either side). It was very unusual to see Lancasters take off in this formation (it was normally associated with fighters) and it was quite a sight – Rear Gunner McDonald from AJ-F in the reserve formation, who were taking off later, looked on disbelievingly.

As the planes took off, Ruth Ive, who was in a Nissen hut at the end of the airfield, felt it rattle and shake as the planes flew over. She had no idea where they were going and the two sergeants who were with her were not letting on – instead they would wait up all night and teach her how to play poker. Humphries waited up with Fay Gillon – he still did not know what his squadron's destination was. Kenneth Lucas of the ground crew on the other hand made his way to bed – he had been working solid for over 24 hours repairing the tail planes on two of the aircraft and would enjoy a very good night's sleep.

There were two more waves of Gibson's flight to take off; the journey over the North Sea would basically be made in three flights of three planes each, flying in close formation. At 2147, 'Dinghy' Young's aircraft (AJ-A) left Scampton along with David Maltby (AJ-J) and Dave Shannon (in AJ-L). Shannon's plane was particularly striking. It had a picture of Bacchus painted on the side in recognition of the crew's capacity to drink enormous amounts of alcohol. These pilots and their crews were mostly experienced flyers but Vivian Nicholson, Maltby's navigator, was on his first operation. Nicholson came from Sherburn, a pit community in County Durham. His father Arthur had a joinery and undertaking business, far from the prestigious social background of some of the other 617 Squadron crew members.

At 2159 Henry Maudslay's plane (AJ-Z) left Scampton along with Bill Astell (AJ-B) and Les Knight (in AJ-M). Struggling sluggishly over the hedge at the end of the runway, the Lancasters climbed cumbrously into the sky, circled once and then disappeared over the horizon. Destiny lay ahead of them, life or death, fame or failure, triumph or tragedy.

The reserve wave would not depart for several hours yet but there was one more plane left to take off. Joe McCarthy had taken command of the spare plane (AJ-T) and had managed to get it into working order. It was all very frantic. Flying Officer Dave Rodger, the rear gunner, bashed out the panel in the rear turret window to improve visibility as the plane prepared to taxi.

Removing the central Perspex window in the rear window was almost routine – it made little difference to the temperature, which was freezing with or without it and only dropped by one degree if this was done, but it seriously increased visibility and therefore chances of survival. On the night, every plane that flew would have the window removed in this way.

McCarthy, over half an hour late, was in a tearing hurry to make up for lost time. In his haste to board the plane he accidentally pulled the ripcord on his parachute, rendering it useless, but at the last moment a spare was handed to him. Humphries thought that he was in such a state that he might make a mess of the take-off but fortunately he did not. A compass deviation card had been fitted but McCarthy would experience serious problems with navigation later on in the flight. There was also a problem with the number three engine, which had led the man who had delivered the aircraft, Commander Bergel, to think that it was unserviceable. Regardless of this, McCarthy now put the plane at full throttle in a desperate attempt to catch up with the wave that he was supposed to be leading.

Having witnessed the departure of the first two waves, the reserve crew in the third returned to their games of poker and waited until it was their turn in a couple of hours' time. For them the wait would have been difficult; they were not even sure where they would be headed for, as this depended on the success or otherwise of the first waves; if the primary targets had not been breached then it would be their job to attempt to complete the task; if not they would be sent to one of the reserve targets. At about 2300 they went to see their ground crews and thanked them for the efforts they had put in and then sat and waited.

In the meantime the first and second waves headed for the English coast and then across the no man's land of the North Sea and the dangers of the German defences facing them on the coast of Europe. There was to be strict RT silence until they crossed the enemy coast. Early on in the flight the aircraft were to drop low over the Wash and test out their spotlights, which were of course critical given the need to drop their weapons from exactly the right height. Maltby tested his at 2210.

The Wash indented the coast of East Anglia and on the other side of it they were back over the land. But at 2219 Gibson's flight crossed the English coast for the last time before reaching the North Sea, Southwold being the departure point. Now they headed towards the darkness, bidding farewell to England, unsure if they would ever see it again.

They were to fly over the North Sea at the very low level of 60 feet and were to set their altimeters at this level, though down that low the instruments were inaccurate and it would be all too easy to make a catastrophic error of judgement. One of the pilots would almost fatally misjudge the altitude that his plane was at and, although he would survive, his mission would be over before it had even really begun.

The second and third wings of this 'first' wave continued on behind. At 2238 'Dinghy' Young crossed the English coast. They too headed for occupied Europe, uncertain of the reception they would find. The element of surprise was all-important and they had to hope that flying at such low heights they would be able to avoid the flak guarding the approaches to Fortress Europe by being past it before the gunners had time to react. They were within an hour of finding out or not whether their luck had held and whether indeed the gods of war were with them.

3

Fortress Europe Attempts to Repel Raids

22.51–23.59, Sunday 16 May

The crossing of the North Sea was uneventful. The waters slipped away behind the raiders with no interruption from enemy aircraft or other scares. It was a deceptively smooth introduction to the events that were about to unfold. Just over an hour after leaving Scampton, the first planes were approaching continental Europe, hoping that they would be through the first line of defences before they were spotted. As they neared the coast, they fused their bombs though they would not be fully armed until released from the plane and dropped on a target.

Perhaps the pre-flight briefing from RAF Tempsford concerning low-level flying particularly started to resonate as the borders of Fortress Europe loomed large. Special Operations Executive missions to land agents in occupied Europe were flown from here and staff there were therefore experts in working out how aircraft could avoid known flak positions. In advance of the raid, 5 Group had asked RAF Tempsford to comment on several proposed routes while trying not to give too much information away about what it was needed for. In an ominous warning, the briefing subsequently prepared had noted that 'from experience it has been found that the time when an aircraft is most likely to be shot at is when crossing the coast'. It was a prediction that would turn out to be distressingly accurate for some of the planes involved in the mission.

Gibson's first wave, as it had a shorter distance to travel, would cross the enemy coast before the wave that was headed for the Sorpe even though it had left later. However, even this early in the flight there were issues with direction-finding.

About five minutes before reaching the coast of Europe, Gibson had received a warning from Torger Taerum that they were approaching enemy-held territory. The spotlights were put on to check their height and they found that they were flying too high at about 100 feet. Flight Sergeant Deering in the front turret got ready to fire back at any flak guns that were insolent enough to try and shoot them down. The tension noticeably tightened a notch or two.

As the coast came into sight, it appeared to Gibson to be 'low and flat and evil' under the spectral light of the moon. They weaved in and out trying to evade the defences they knew were there which had been as fully mapped out as possible in advance. Gibson thought the planes seemed like ships trying to pick their way through a minefield. They roared over the Western Wall, initially catching the defences off guard. However, they had not yet crossed the coast proper, merely an island just off it, and were soon back over the sea once more, though not for long before reaching the mainland.

At 2252 Gibson and the first group crossed the Scheldt Estuary. He was slightly south-west of where he should have been and had crossed Walcheren Island instead of passing between here and the island of Schouewen as he should have done. This was not good as Walcheren was strongly defended. Unsure of where he was, Gibson climbed to 300 feet to orientate himself properly. Once up at this height, Navigator Taerum calculated a revised heading.

As Gibson turned left to get himself back on track, 'Hoppy' Hopgood lost sight of him and they flew on out of sight of each other. The fact that crews were off course even as soon as they reached the Continent hinted at the difficulties that lay ahead for the raiders. The areas they were to pass through to reach the dams were heavily defended and the smallest of errors could lead them into trouble as they flew into heavy flak. A margin of just a mile or so could mean the difference between life and death, as some of the crews would soon find out.

Gibson was fortunate to escape the flak of the coastal defences without harm. His plane had sprung out of the darkness over the coast and caught the gunners off their guard. They flew on, so low that more than once they were forced to suddenly shoot up in the air to avoid trees or high-tension cables. They then came across a canal, which was to be a point of reference for them to follow, and had soon reached a turning point at which they were to divert towards the Rhine. The canals were indeed godsends in terms of finding where they were.

This was helpful but it was an inherent problem of such low flying that it was very difficult to navigate accurately. In the dark the planes were often past a landmark before they even realised they were there. The moonlight helped with more obvious markers such as rivers and canals, but many others were hard to identify as the planes shot past objects that would, in the daylight, have been much easier to pick out.

Gibson would not hit problems with flak until he reached Germany proper, where he later had to take evasive action. With a dozen searchlights illuminating the sky over enemy territory, Gibson and his crew felt very conspicuous but he managed to weave his way in and out of the gunfire without being hit. At these low heights, heavy flak – 88- and 105-mm Anti-Aircraft (AA) guns – would be ineffective as the planes would be past them before they could home in on them. However, 20-mm guns would be a definite threat – these could fire at 120 rounds a minute and were more than capable of hitting low-flying aircraft. The British pilots just had to hope that their sudden arrival without warning would catch the gunners off-guard.

Martin described the threat from the flak rather well: 'from 7,000 feet upwards there was so-called heavy flak, and down to 3,000 feet there were night fighters. From 200 feet up to 4,000 feet there was light flak. Below 200 feet it's hard to hear low-flying aircraft approaching and it's damned difficult for ground gunners – if they did hear – to swing on and lay off the necessary deflection.' Such was the hope and for some of them it would be fulfilled; some but not all.

The route had anyway been carefully planned to avoid flak as much as possible. Tempsford had recommended key points along the track to particularly watch out for. A certain degree of precision was required; for example, the northern route should fly over the middle of the island of Vlieland as there were flak positions at either end. This confirmed that margins of error were extremely small.

Landmarks were carefully chosen on the route too, in an attempt to help the crews stay on track; water features were especially useful for this purpose. The bomb-aimer was to remain face down in the nose for the entire trip to assist with navigation, which cannot have made for a comfortable mission.

If Gibson's wave was to escape unscathed from their crossing of the coast, the same was not true of the planes of the second wave over a hundred miles to the north. At 2255, just a few minutes after Gibson had crossed over miles to the south, Flight Lieutenant Robert Barlow in AJ-E was the first of the northern wave to reach the Continent, passing over the coast of the Netherlands. He was fortunate to catch the AA defences off their guard. His comrades would not be so lucky.

A minute later Les Munro in AJ-W fused his bomb. Another minute passed and then Pilot Officer Geoffrey Rice in AJ-H was aware of an explosion lighting up the sky. It was the sight of the plane of Pilot Officer Vernon Byers being hit by gunfire.

Byers was just off the coast of the Netherlands when his plane was hit by gunfire from the coastal defences guarding the approaches to continental Europe. It was a fatal blow. The bomber crashed into the sea off the island of Vlieland, one of the chain of isles shielding the Netherlands from the North Sea. There were no survivors. Only one body was found, that of Sergeant James McDowell, who was a gunner. He was later buried with dignity in the General Cemetery at Harlington. It was the worst possible start. The Sorpe flight had not even reached the mainland and the first plane had been lost.

Byers was a Canadian and, at thirty-two years of age, one of the oldest men flying that night. He had passed through 1654 Conversion Unit earlier that year, where he had got to know 'Mick' Martin, who was an instructor there. Despite his maturity, Byers was a very recent recruit, having joined the RCAF in 1941. He had then passed through 1654 Conversion Unit, where he had flown with Mick Martin on four occasions. Following that, he had been posted to 467 Squadron on 5 February 1943, where he spent only seven weeks before being moved to 617 Squadron. He had had a relatively short and fatally unlucky stint as a bomber pilot.

The route of this wave headed for the Sorpe was planned to take a path over the island of Vlieland. However, in the dying light it would be difficult to distinguish this from its southerly neighbour, Texel, which was very heavily defended. The wind that night was stronger than forecast and may have driven the planes slightly off course to the south. This had already led to potential danger for Gibson himself as he could have found out over the heavily defended island of Walcheren if his luck had not been in.

Byers had been seen gaining height, a hint that he was unsure of his correct position and was climbing to try and establish it. This led to danger; at very low levels the planes would be over the defences before the gun crews on anti-aircraft duty had spotted them. At any rate, only light guns could be manoeuvred into position quickly enough to get a shell away at the planes going over. But once the aircraft rose higher up, even marginally so, they would be vulnerable.

The Dutch Frisian islands chain was defended by seven batteries of AA guns from Marine-Flakabteilung 246 of the German Navy. RAF Intelligence believed that this area was lightly defended. Where the shell that brought Byers down was fired from remains a matter of debate. The intended route took the wave just north of Vlieland, well out of reach of the guns around the Dutch naval base at Den Helder. Some argue that the defences of Texel were responsible for bringing the plane down, suggesting that it was to the south of where it should have been – a not impossible suggestion given the conditions that night. However, experts who have studied the matter now believe that there were no gun emplacements on the north of the island that could have been responsible for bringing Byers down.

The gap between Texel and Den Helder on the mainland also looked quite similar to that between Vlieland and Texel, so it would be easy for a pilot to mistake their position. The fact that Byers crashed in the sea means that it is virtually impossible to be sure who was responsible for bringing him down (a crash over land would at least allow some educated guesswork as to where the gun was fired from). However, a convincing candidate for the unit that fired the decisive shot was the aforementioned Marine-Flakabteilung 246, which was based on the western side of Vlieland.

There were fractions between life and death, surviving or not, and there were three elements in particular that were responsible for whether a crew would return. The first was the skill of the pilot, the second the intensity of the training that the men had been through, the third plain old-fashioned luck. Some of the crew later thanked their lucky stars for the pilots whom they depended on so much. Sergeant Basil Feneron, the flight engineer in AJ-F, spoke glowingly of how 'Ken Brown always kept us up to scratch. He used to take us away to knock seconds off dinghy and escape drills, while a lot of crews were more interested in the birds they were taking out.' Such skill and dedication could keep men alive.

It was only a matter of moments before another plane from this northern wave was in trouble. At 2257 Munro's aircraft was damaged by fire from a flak-ship off the coast. His radio equipment was knocked out (in fact, the transmitter, intercom and master compass were all damaged) and as he was unable to communicate with other aircraft he had to consider whether to abort his mission or not. A note was passed around to seek views from the crew – the damage meant the intercom was useless. The bomb-aimer, Jim Clay, suggested they would just get in the way of everyone else if they carried on.

Munro later insisted that his plane had only suffered one hit but it was nevertheless decisive as far as his involvement in the raids was concerned. The pilot circled his plane around at a safe distance from the flak while his wireless operator, Flying Officer Percy Pigeon, was sent to look at the damage and see if it could be repaired. He soon reported back that the equipment was unfixable; with no intercom between the crew, effective communication even inside the plane would be very difficult. For a higher-altitude raid, with more time to work out an alternative system, something might have been possible but on this low-level mission, where everything was happening so fast, it was impossible. The master compass unit was also destroyed. It was a litany of problems which in the end forced Munro to take the decision to abort.

Even as all this action was happening, back at base everyone was in the dark as yet as to how the raid was going. For them, it was effectively the calm before the storm. Everything that could have been done had now been done – all they could do was to wait to find out how successful they had been. At 2300 Wallis, Cochrane, Harris and other luminaries left Scampton for Grantham, where they would later be able to receive news as it was Morsed in. Several hours of tortured waiting were to follow. Only about now was there complete darkness over Western Europe as the short late May night began.

It was as well perhaps that those at Scampton were metaphorically in the dark as to what was going on as far as the wave of planes headed for the Sorpe dam was concerned. This part of the mission was already threatening to turn into an unmitigated disaster. At 2259 Pilot Officer Geoffrey Rice in plane AJ-H was about to reach the Continent. All of a sudden, panic reigned on his aircraft. Sergeant Edward Smith, the flight engineer, noted that the barometric altimeter read zero.

It almost exactly the same moment, Rice became terribly aware that the water beneath him was looming up far too closely. He had misjudged the altitude that he was flying at and was about to hit the sea. As he struggled to gain height at the last second he clipped the waves and water started to come into the plane. So much entered that the deluge threatened to drown Sergeant Sandy Burns in the rear turret as it poured down towards the back of the plane before cascading out.

Rice's instinctive reaction saved the plane and the crew as it zoomed up on an upward trajectory, but the bomb hanging from the bomb-bay was torn out and lost by the impact of the collision with the water. Burns shouted out, 'Christ! It's wet at the back ...' followed by, 'You've lost the mine!' Burns was in danger of being drowned before the water drained out of the rear turret as the plane climbed higher; he was fortunate to survive.

The loss of the bomb from Rice's aircraft meant that there was absolutely no point in continuing with the mission. In addition, Rice lost both outboard engines and there was even a doubt about whether or not he could make it back to England. In the event, he limped back to England on his two inboard engines. When they eventually arrived back at Scampton, Burns had to be cut out of the rear turret in which he was trapped.

The collision emphasised the dangers of low flying. It has been suggested that perhaps the lights that were supposed to be used to gauge the correct height had been set incorrectly and caused Rice to fly too low. Whatever the true reason, it was a powerful reminder of just how dangerous this mission was.

Rice would not be returning alone. At 2306 Bill Howarth, the front turret gunner in Munro's aircraft (AJ-W), felt the plane bank and realised that they were also returning home. Munro too had decided to abort his mission. Unlike Rice, he was going back with his bomb still dangling out from the callipers in the bomb-bay. This was specifically against Gibson's orders. However, Munro would not be reprimanded in any way for his actions. This contrasted somewhat with the treatment of one other pilot who returned home with his bomb undropped.

This was a terrible start for the mission on the Sorpe. There had already been doubts expressed before the raids as to the viability of breaching the dam there, and now, of the five planes deputed to attack it (already one short after Divall's late withdrawal), one had been shot down and two others were limping back to base within minutes of reaching the Continent. Further, the leader of this wave had not even crossed the coast yet. It was a sorry tale and it was not going to improve any time soon.

For Gibson at least the initial crossing of the coast had gone relatively smoothly so far. At 2303 his plane passed Roosendal. He soon after picked up the helpful signposting offered by the Wilhelmina canal below him; following this he was able to avoid the heavy AA defences of a Luftwaffe base north of Eindhoven, which was more fortunate than some of his colleagues behind him would be.

In the meantime, the next group in his wave was, at 2312, crossing the Scheldt Estuary. This was the group including Squadron Leader Melvyn Young's Lancaster (AJ-A), Flight Lieutenant David Maltby's AJ-J and Flight Lieutenant Dave Shannon in AJ-L. Unlike Gibson's flight, they had arrived on track and did not, as he had been forced to do, need to run the gauntlet of the heavy defences on Walcheren.

Yet in many ways their problems had only just begun. While they had breached the first line of defence successfully, they were now flying low over enemy territory and this was an extremely dangerous part of the journey. Both the front gunner and the bomb-aimer had a crucial role in looking out for obstructions ahead as, in addition to avoiding flak positions, they also had to avoid obstacles like pylons, church towers and trees that might bring them down at any moment.

The route had been chosen with several objectives in mind. One of them was to avoid all known flak positions. The other was to have relatively short distances between waymarks on the route to enable the planes to regularly check out their position and make sure that they were in the right place. Despite this, several planes in the southern wave had to take evasive action from flak on the way in.

In the meantime, further north, Joe McCarthy had been flying flat out to catch up with the rest of his flight, unaware that, with the exception of one other plane that was ploughing onwards, it had now effectively ceased to exist. By 2313 he had reached Vlieland (this was just a minute after Young, Maltby and Shannon had crossed the coast of Europe 100 miles further south with Maudslay, Astell and Knight 10 minutes behind). This shows something of the speed he was going at. Though he had left Scampton 33 minutes after the first plane in the Sorpe wave, he was crossing the coast only 18 minutes behind; this was symptomatic of a man in a hurry.

The gunners on Vlieland were now wide awake, having been made aware of the threat by the four planes that had already tried to break through their defences, only one of which had succeeded. As a result, there was a hot reception but McCarthy was able to fly in between two sand dunes which offered some protection and allowed him to escape.

As McCarthy flew on, he spotted a goods train. Ron Batson, the front gunner, asked for permission to attack it, which was granted. This turned out to be a mistake; it was an armoured train which fired back rather more fiercely than anticipated. The plane was hit, though not badly. It was only much later, when they landed back at Scampton, that they found out where damage had been done: the starboard tyre had been burst.

Navigation for all the planes remained difficult. Don MacLean, McCarthy's navigator, did not use the roll map method whereby the maps were laid out in a long roll that was unwound as the journey progressed; he thought that it was useless if the plane went off course (only a narrow corridor on the route had been incorporated in the roll maps) so instead they took ordinary maps and used them as needed, which took up much more room but were more useful if the aircraft went astray at all.

Neither were the raiders solely in danger from flak. Night fighters from the Luftwaffe base at Leeuwarden, east of the Ijsselmeer, had been deployed to engage the bombers whose presence was now known. However, night flying was a relatively new discipline. The fighters had a very limited radar range and the fact that the British were flying at low levels meant that they were not spotted by the fighters who were flying high above them. McCarthy said that he could frequently see the planes flying about 1,000 feet higher than him but they could clearly not see him. Some of the fighters would be in the air for nearly two hours but not one would come close to intercepting anyone from 617 Squadron.

Gibson too continued to head for his target. By 2322 he had passed Beek. Here the Wilhelmina canal ended and they headed east-north-east across largely featureless countryside where, in the absence of clear landmarks, the plane once more drifted off course to the south. When he soon spotted the unmistakable outline of the Rhine below him, Gibson once more adjusted his course and tried to get back on track, but in the process he also lost contact with Martin.

Martin was also doing his best to stay on track. It was surprising, alarming even, how quite mundane matters interfered when flying at such low levels. His windscreen was splattered with spray from the sea and dead bugs; the latter were especially difficult to distinguish from landmarks on the route.

By 2325 Young had passed Roosendal, distinguishable from the air by the large railway junction to the north of the town, about 20 minutes behind Gibson. He then headed slightly to the left, passing south of Breda and Tilburg, where soon after the line of the Wilhelmina canal would be followed. This should take the planes between the heavily defended airfields of Gilze-Rijen on the left and Eindhoven on the right. After Eindhoven, another canal would be reached at the village of Beek. Then from Rees the planes, by now in German airspace, would fly to a group of lakes near Dulmen.

That something was afoot was now obvious to the Germans. Even those close to the dams were alerted. At 2330 the inhabitants of Günne, the village at the very foot of the Möhne dam, heard an air-raid warning. One of the residents was a special constable, Ferdinand Nölle, who recalled that 'after the war began, for some time before the raid, people in Neheim [the nearest town downstream] started to phone in to complain. They said we should let some of the water out so as to reduce the danger if there was a raid. But nothing happened.' The residents of Neheim had every reason to be nervous of what might occur should the dam be breached.

However, it was still not at all obvious where the planes in the air on this particular full-moon night were headed. At 2334 Gibson passed Rees. Near here, his flight met with a hostile reception from flak. The three planes in his flight, now separated, returned fire with interest and managed to pass the defences undamaged. Further gunfire would be experienced near Dorsten and also near Dülmen. The closer they got to the heart of Germany, the more unfriendly the reception would become.

As Gibson's crew flew on, they realised that again they had strayed off course and had come too close to the heavily defended town of Duisburg, a significant industrial centre and therefore well guarded. Taerum took responsibility for this error as he had calculated the wrong course; Gibson reminded him that this could be 'an expensive mistake'. Although this might seem harsh, in this instance it was justified as Taerum needed to be on his guard. He did not seem to be having a good night and further errors could be fatal.

They were also approaching a particularly dangerous area in terms of German defences. As they passed deeper into the Ruhr valley, the flak guns homed in on Gibson and the other planes in his flight. Searchlights lit up the sky and guns spat out at the aircraft, but their low height was a bonus, making it difficult for the gunners to get an accurate fix on a plane in time. On occasion, Gibson was even screened by the trees that loomed up beside his aircraft.

They flew on, past Dortmund and Hamm, the latter a very frequent target for bombing activity with its large rail-marshalling yards. Then they moved past Soest, the main administrative centre for the region around the Möhne dam, where Gibson had almost been shot down three years before. It was sleepy now and the guns, if there were any there, were quiet – a welcome change since the last time he was in the area. Then ahead of them they saw the gentle hills above the Möhne dam. The target zone was almost in sight.

But navigation was becoming increasingly difficult. At 2342, Sergeant Vivian Nicholson, Maltby's navigator, noted that the Gee system was 'jammed something chronic', which was to be expected now that the planes were moving towards the end of Gee's effective range. Other operators commented favourably on the system in the early parts of the raid, saying that it worked well until they got into Germany; but Dudley Heal, Ken Brown's navigator in the reserve wave, also later found that it jammed. The German counter-defences against this equipment were proving especially effective.

Gibson's wave had at least so far managed to avoid damage from flak, but their luck was about to turn. Nearby, 'Hoppy' Hopgood was also headed for problems. One moment rear gunner Burcher was thinking of his bride-to-be – he was due to be married next month – the next moment he felt his stomach metaphorically hit the ground as the Lancaster he was in took sharp evasive action. A high-tension wire loomed ahead and Hopgood had to take a split-second decision to avoid it. He was flying so low that he actually flew underneath it.

When the plane was picked up by searchlights. Gunfire spat out angrily at them. At 2345, while flying over Dülmen, 'Hoppy' Hopgood's plane was badly shot up. His rear gunner, Pilot Officer Anthony Burcher, noticed a strong smell of cordite in the plane. The port outer engine had been hit and was aflame: Flight Engineer Sgt Charles Brennan shut down the damaged Merlin and feathered the propeller. Hopgood though managed to regain power and gamely headed on towards the Möhne.

But the plane had been badly hit. Burcher felt blood in his mouth, but he would be one of the luckier casualties that night. Sergeant John

Minchin, the wireless operator, was hit and badly wounded; he could not move his leg. There was no response from Pilot Officer George Gregory in the front turret and Burcher assumed that he was dead. Hopgood was also badly injured: blood was streaming from his head and Charles Brennan, the flight engineer, had to tend to his wounds.

Hopgood at least managed to head on, still carrying his weapon and still able to take his part in the mission. But further to the north, the wave headed for the Sorpe was about to suffer another disastrous reverse. 'Norm' Barlow, an Australian pilot flying in AJ-E, had developed a well-deserved reputation as a survivor, having nursed back a damaged plane to base on more than one occasion. Now, though, his luck had run out.

He was an experienced pilot, unusual in being in his thirties, old for those taking part in the raids. He was the first of the 'Dambusters' to take off and had managed to fly without damage over the Netherlands. But then at 2350, when over Germany near Haldern (north of Rees), he all of a sudden found himself suddenly in danger of being ensnared by high-tension power cables. It was too late to avoid them. Staggering on for a few hundred yards into a field, the plane hit the ground and went up in flames. The impact was shattering, so much so that there were no survivors. Now, of the five planes in this northern wave, only one was left to attempt to breach the Sorpe dam: the one flown by the resilient Joe McCarthy.

Among the dead in Barlow's crew was Jack Liddell, the youngest crew member that night. He had previously been thrown out of the RAF as he had lied about his age when he joined up, aged just fifteen. Disappointed, he instead became a member of the Fire Service during the London Blitz. He later re-enlisted and was given the ironic name of 'killer' – he was a gunner but had never fired his guns in anger.

Barlow's bomb miraculously did not detonate and was recovered intact by the Germans, a wonderful gift for them which meant that all security measures that had been taken to keep the device a secret were largely superfluous. There would be little point in taking further measures to keep the device a secret when the Germans had a fully functional model in their hands.

Even before it was light the next day the local people gathered around the bomb, wondering what exactly this strangely shaped object might be. The mayor of Haldern was one of the crowd, the consensus among which was that this was a large petrol canister. This encouraged the mayor to quip that 'I'll tell the Chief Administrative

Officer that he needn't send us any more petrol coupons for the rest of the war.' At one stage he even climbed on top of it and had his photograph taken. He was later reported to have felt decidedly queasy when told that it was in fact full of high explosive.

Only a few personal possessions were salvaged from the wreck site: cases, gold rings and a torch on which the number of missions that the owner had flown – thirty-two – was recorded. There were also the names of towns including Palermo scratched into it. This was a pitifully small collection of objects to mark the snuffing out of seven lives.

By the following morning the bomb was being examined and within a month a preliminary report concerning it was on the desk of Albert Speer. Detailed descriptions of the bomb were distributed to, among others, Hermann Goering. The descriptions noted, for example, the precise dimensions of the device and the presence of the hydrostatic pistols. In fact there were three of these pistols fitted so that if one were damaged on impact, one of the other two at least would hopefully work. These were based on standard Admiralty design and were what made the device a depth-charge rather than a bomb or a mine.

With the Sorpe attack now almost doomed to fail as just one plane from the designated wave was left to deliver the attack, all hopes for making a significant impact on the Ruhr industries rested on Gibson's flight. They headed on relentlessly towards their appointment with destiny. The flak as they flew through the Ruhr valley had been very active, though by weaving and jinking most of it was avoided. Searchlights had picked up planes from time to time, but because they were flying so low it was hard for the lights to stay on the aircraft; a number of the searchlights continued to be dodged by hopping behind trees.

Despite all the odds, Gibson and the eight planes behind him pushed on remorselessly. Now the major defences were behind them, and just a few miles and even fewer minutes in front of them was the dam that was their primary target. With midnight approaching, a poignant scene was even now being played out back at Scampton. Gibson's beloved pet was being interred in the cold earth of the airbase, beneath his office, buried with all the dignity that could be mustered. Nigger's grave was in front of No. 2 hangar and a simple wooden cross had been made by one of the 'chippies' to mark the spot.

For all his single-mindedness, perhaps for a brief second Gibson's mind wandered back over the miles to think one last farewell to his old friend. Perhaps too he thought he might soon be joining him. Within an hour he would either be a hero or he would be dead. Perhaps after all he might be both.

4

Attack on Möhne: Early Attacks Over Target X & Target Z

00.00–00.30, Monday 17 May

The first wave was now drawing close to the Möhne dam. With the exception of the damage done to Hopgood's plane, Gibson's flight had escaped relatively lightly so far. To near the dam with a full complement of planes was better than can have been hoped for and in marked contrast to what had happened to the wave headed for the Sorpe.

However, reconnaissance had shown that the dam was defended by flak and this meant that the attack was unlikely to be as straightforward as those against the others, where there were believed to be no anti-aircraft guns in place. But even for Gibson's flight, the closer they got to the heart of the Ruhr, the more resistance they were likely to experience. At 0007, John Minchin, Hopgood's wireless operator, transmitted a warning of flak over to the east of Dulmen. By now, Hopgood's crew were well aware of how dangerous the flak was.

The other two flights of this wave were continuing to make good progress behind Gibson. At 0009, 'Dinghy' Young, in the first-wave flight behind Gibson, reached the Dulmen waypoint. Here, following the pre-planned route, they turned right heading for Ahlen, where there was a prominent railway line to follow. Again, it was important to have clearly visible landmarks to point the way.

With the first wave almost at its destination, it was high time that the reserve planes were despatched from back at Scampton. They could be informed of their ultimate destination when they were en route, dependent on the success of Gibson's wave in pushing home their attack. There was no doubt that the Möhne dam was the number one objective; but after that, everything was much less clear, as would become apparent later on.

Accordingly, at 0009, Pilot Officer Warner Ottley in AJ-C left Scampton, the first of the reserve wave to take off. Two minutes later, Pilot Officer Lewis Burpee in AJ-S was next up, followed a minute later by Ken Brown in AJ-F. They made their way towards the Continent and would pick up further instructions en route. Just before take-off, Burpee had gone over to Brown, his fellow Canadian, thrust out his hand and said laconically 'goodbye Ken'. Brown took his hand and shook it; he knew that this mission was far from a 'sure bet'.

It is interesting to note that all three NCO pilots were in this third reserve wave and this has led some historians to speculate that this may have been because they were considered of inferior standing, both socially and in terms of experience, to those in the first and second wave. Yet both Townsend and Brown would prove themselves to be top-notch pilots during the raids. In fact, in some ways this reserve wave, which does not appear to have been as well briefed on some of the targets as the first and second waves and also had to be flexible enough to attack any one of a number of possible targets – their specific objective would only be advised later in the raid – perhaps had the hardest job of all.

Brown later recalled that, understandably, 'we were all frightened'. The nerves had had plenty of time to develop once the first two waves had left two and a half hours previously. There was so much time to brood once the fourteen planes of the first two waves had gone and for dark thoughts to enter the minds of these men hanging around with time on their hands, facing one of the most dangerous nights of their lives. But for them, at last the waiting had come to an end. Now they were taken out in a bus to the planes, three crews to each vehicle. Brown's crew were the third to disembark.

As the first two crews got off the bus and walked the few yards to their aircraft, Brown's rear gunner went very quiet and then said to him, 'You know those two crews aren't coming back, don't you?' Brown replied in the affirmative. Sadly, this information was correct; both crews would be dead within two hours. There was something in the manner of crews that knew they were about to die, a quietness in their attitude which hinted at a certain knowledge of their impending doom.

Such sixth senses were not unheard of in such life and death situations and turned out to be accurate and prescient surprisingly often. Brown presumably did not suffer from the same heavy burden of a sense of his own impending doom but his departure from Scampton was difficult. There was no wind as the plane was taking off, which worried Brown as he felt they needed all the assistance going to get their heavy load off the ground. To him, the hedge at the end of the runway looked a thousand feet tall.

Flight Sergeant Bill Townsend in AJ-O left Scampton at 0014 and just a minute later Flight Sergeant Cyril Anderson and his crew in AJ-Y were the very last to take off. It was much darker now and the moon was past its zenith, which meant that it would be harder to see reflected light on the water en route and over the targets and navigation would be more difficult. As the night went on, this would turn out to be a major problem for Anderson and his crew in particular.

By now, Gibson was nearly at the primary target. Approaching the Möhne dam, his first wave had experienced difficulties with Hopgood's plane being shot up but still able to carry on. Behind, the other two flights in the first wave were still on course too. At 0012, Henry Maudslay's section, the third flight in Gibson's wave, made the turn at Rees and headed east. Les Knight turned with him but Bill Astell may have got confused at this point. It was now that the first wave hit further, more serious problems.

Flying Officer Harold Hobday on AJ-N (Knight's plane) had noticed that someone – Bill Astell – had strayed off too far to the right and moved away from him in an effort to make sure that he did not follow suit. This was a particularly difficult part of the route. Knight's plane suddenly came dangerously close to a pylon and just managed to avoid it; Astell was not so lucky.

In a farmhouse close to Marbeck, the residents were awoken by the sounds of aircraft flying at a very low altitude. Air raids were not unusual in the region and there was in fact a warning of one in force at the time. On many nights, they could see the airspace over the Ruhr lit up from the effect of the bombs that had rained down there. But this plane was unusually low and attracted their attention.

One of the residents ran out, just in time to see that a plane had crashed into a pylon and gone up in flames. It was Bill Astell's aircraft, which had been so low that it had almost scraped the roof of a farmhouse before hitting the pylon. The top of the pylon had been thrown off into a neighbour's yard. Everything was lit up by the burning plane, ammunition was exploding left, right and centre. The witness watched as a fiery ball burst from the wreckage and rolled about 150 metres away from the plane. It was a terrifying fiery inferno.

Even as the residents looked on in disbelief, there was a fierce explosion that shook the house to its very foundations. Only after half an hour was it possible to brave the heat of the inferno and approach the plane. When one of the bystanders did so, he could see a man in a crouched position, leaning on his hands. He was completely charred and stiff, a horrible sight. On the edge of the massive bomb crater, eyewitnesses saw several young airmen, all without outward signs of injury but all dead. Within a radius of 3 kilometres, roofs had been blown off houses, doors thrown off hinges and windows shattered in the terrific explosion that had followed the crash. The bomb had rolled about 100 yards away from the blazing plane and then gone up in a huge eruption.

This brought to a premature end an eventful and adventurous flying career. Bill Astell was born in 1920 into an upper-class family in Cheshire. He had spent much of his adolescence travelling. He began his RAF flying career in Egypt in 1941, where he flew Wellingtons. A crash in November of that year left him hospitalised for three months. Returning to duty in March the next year, he failed to return from a mission over enemy territory in May and was reported as missing in action in the conventional telegram to his family. However, he turned up five days later having crash-landed and been later picked up by Arabs.

Astell had been posted to 57 Squadron at Scampton in January 1943, when he started flying in Lancasters. Five of Astell's crew had trained together at 1654 Conversion Unit at Wigsley, being posted together to 9 Squadron on 23 December 1942. Three of them were Canadians. This time there would be no return from the dead: Astell and all his crew had gone. A local policeman later examined the site and meticulously listed any items that had survived: money, a ring, a watch, a cigarette case, keys – a pathetic but poignant set of relics that was all that remained along with bodies, some of which could not be identified, to evidence seven more lives now lost.

But there was one object left undamaged. Just 50 metres from the bomb crater was a statue of St Joseph with the baby Jesus in his arms. This was completely untouched by the explosion while buildings further away were damaged. Many of the locals were inclined to think this was something of a miracle.

Even as Astell and his crew were meeting their tragic end behind him, Gibson had at last reached the airspace above the Möhne dam (Martin was already there). His job now was not to move straight into the attack but to wait to coordinate the assault as the master bomber. So his plane settled in an anti-clockwise holding pattern 10 kilometres south of Völlinghausen and waited for the other planes in the first wave to catch up.

A few miles away, those responsible for the defence of the Möhne dam were still unaware that they were the intended target. The dam wall was defended by 3. Batterie/Leichte Flak-Abteilung 840 equipped with six single-barrelled 20-mm automatic cannon. Two of these were on top of the sluice towers, one on the balcony on the north side of the dam and three to the north below the dam. The guns fired armour-piercing high-explosive shells at a rate of 200 rounds a minute. Although the guns were theoretically effective at a range of up to 7,218 feet – just over a mile – in practice fire was normally commenced at a range of 3,280 feet.

The Germans at the Möhne dam were completely oblivious of the attack that was about to hit them; it had been a quiet night and a normal watch of unalleviated mundane inactivity. There was no noise. But then the silence was broken by a phone ringing. They heard that an alarm had been sounded at nearby Lünn Castle. The gun crews were alerted and prepared to resist any attackers. They soon grew bored again, thinking that this was a false alarm, but were shaken from their lethargy by the sound of engines to the north coming from the direction of Soest. Maybe they might see some action after all.

Just a few miles to the south, also at 0015, Joe McCarthy had reached the vicinity of the Sorpe dam. The absence of other planes was a worry; he had after all been the last to leave. He was supposed to be the leader of this second wave which had been deputed to attack the Sorpe dam, but there were no other planes to lead. McCarthy's plane had been shot at by a battery of five 20-mm guns close to the Sorpe, but he and his crew now had the dam to themselves.

However, there were other problems facing McCarthy besides the lack of supporting planes. It was already quite misty when McCarthy reached the Sorpe. They were attacking the dam longways on, so that meant flying down the side of one steep hill and quickly up that of another on the other side of the dam; no easy task, this was flying that called for both skill and nerve. McCarthy positioned himself above the village of Langscheid to get into the right position for his assault. As he looked down far below onto the 2,100-foot-long earthen dam, he remarked, 'Jeez! How do we get down there?'

There was a church steeple in the way at the top of the hill on the way in, unexpected as it had not been identified in briefings (this is a surprise as it is quite an obvious landmark), which they hurriedly had to avoid. It was right at the crest and close to the run-in to the dam, an awkward obstacle but in its own way a useful marker for the final approach. It would take about three seconds from the moment that McCarthy dropped down to the dam below to the moment he reached the correct position to drop his bomb. This would be an incredibly difficult task.

Those attacking the Sorpe had a different allocated VHF radio frequency to those attacking the Möhne, but as it happened this was superfluous for there was no one there with McCarthy and anyway his reserve plane that had been delivered at the last minute did not have the VHF fitted as there had not been time to do so.

Precision was called for if there were to be any chance of breaching the Sorpe dam. The massive earth bank would cushion the explosion and even before the raids there had been much less confidence that the attack here would be a success. But it had been calculated that the bomb should be dropped as near as possible to the centre of the dam and about 20 feet out from it so that it could roll down the water side of the earthen wall and explode at 30 feet below the surface.

The design of the dam necessitated a different approach as it had gently sloping banks (though they were much steeper on the air side as opposed to the water side) rather than vertical walls. If the angle of attack had been the same as that employed at the Möhne and later the Eder dams, the high level of the water and the gentle slopes of the dam walls would probably have resulted in the bomb bouncing harmlessly over the top of the dam (though the power station below might have been wiped out as the one at the Möhne reservoir had). Therefore the approach was to be to fly along the dam rather than come in at right angles to it.

Given the drop down the hill that needed to be made when the attack was launched, and the hurried exit that would then be required once the weapon had been dropped, it would be very hard to release the bomb in exactly the right spot. To help him, McCarthy decided to use the church tower as a marker. They had been briefed to line up the port engine with the dam wall. But the task would be every bit as challenging as it appeared; it would take ten runs over the dam before McCarthy was happy with his dropping position.

The attack on the Sorpe was far less well rehearsed than those on the Möhne and Eder dams. Bomb-aimer George Johnson recalled that 'we had no practice on our type of attack on the Sorpe at all. We didn't know in fact what kind of attack it was going to be until the briefing. That gave us the style of attack, but the actual geography of it we didn't know until we got to the Sorpe. All our practising had been with the bouncing-bomb method at right angles to the objective. None of it had been running along the line of a dam wall.' This suggests a certain lack of cohesion, maybe even confidence, in the attack on the Sorpe dam. The attack on the dam here was completely under-rehearsed compared to that on the Möhne.

Down below, some residents of the isolated community up in the hills by the Sorpe dam were already getting nervous. Josef Kesting, a machinist, was asleep in his accommodation at the Sorpe power station, at the base of the earth dam, when his wife woke him up. She told him, 'You'd better get up, a plane keeps flying over.'

Kesting went outside to investigate, where he found that several of his workmates had already gathered, also alerted by the strange actions of an aircraft in the area. Even as he looked he saw a plane approaching very low. It flew past him, less than 100 metres off. He could clearly see the distinctive rings of an English aircraft painted on the side. This not unnaturally alarmed him and he ran inside, telling his wife to grab their son and go down into the cellar of one of the company flats at the base of the dam. This would of course be one of the worst places they could have been in should the dam walls be breached.

At the same time, the planes were now starting to assemble a few miles away at the Möhne dam even as, at 0016, Les Munro was arriving back over the English coast having nursed his damaged plane safely homewards. Four minutes later, Young identified Ahlen down below. His plane turned right (south-south-east), passing between the towns of Werl and Soest, where he was required to take more evasive action from flak.

As the planes moved down towards the Möhne reservoir, they

got their first view of the challenge facing them. As well as the six guns placed on or near the dam, there were two anti-torpedo nets in front of it, some 6 feet apart and going down to a depth of 15 metres beneath the surface. The Germans clearly believed that this was more than sufficient to prevent any successful attack that might be attempted. There were no balloons over the dam to deter any planes though artificial trees had been placed on it to try and offer some basic camouflage; but this did nothing to deceive an attacking plane in practice (they were in fact a framework covered by netting to make them look like trees). The lack of searchlights at the Möhne dam suggested a degree of complacency on the part of the Germans, as if they could not believe that it would ever be attacked.

There were some interested observers who were about to get a grandstand view of the action that was about to unfold. A party of grammar school boys from Soest had spent the day at the lake and had stopped overnight at a hostel at Delecke on its northern shore. There were no adults supervising them overnight as so many of the teachers had been called up. The boys had enjoyed a pleasant evening and were listening to 'Lili Marlene' on a portable gramophone. It was as far away from a war zone as anyone was likely to be in Germany in 1943. It was a beautiful spot on the shores of the lake, where the only distraction during the course of the day had been the lazy flying of herons overhead.

The record had just finished when there was another noise that could be heard, this one more ominous and threatening: the low humming of engines. Then the noise grew louder until, almost overhead, it was deafening. The boys ran outside to watch and would look on spellbound on a succession of planes heading over them and low across the lake until the aircraft disappeared behind a narrow spit of land that hid the dam from the boys. Delecke, where there was a road bridge across the lake, was in an inlet and they would not therefore be able to see the dam from there. However, they would have had a grandstand view of any planes that flew in to attack the dam until the crucial last few moments before the bombs were released.

Special Constable Ferdinand Nölle was on duty on the dam itself. He was supposed to be relieved by Wilhelm Strotkamp at 0020 but the latter was not there on time. When Strotkamp did at last arrive, Nölle asked him why he was so late. Strotkamp explained to him that 'I've been watching the show over on the water side.' Matters were about to take a dramatic turn.

At 0023, Gibson decided to make a dummy run on the dam. This might alert the defences on the dam itself but it had to be done so that the dangers of any forthcoming action could be better assessed. Having successfully completed this dry run, he remarked, 'I like the look of it.' Just three minutes later, 'Dinghy' Young had reached the vicinity of the Möhne dam, though of the planes in his flight Dave Shannon was slightly behind the others. David Maltby also arrived at about this time and soon all the planes of the first wave, minus Bill Astell and his crew, were now ready for action.

The VHF radio sets were switched on and preparations were now made to use them in the attack. They were only to be switched on ten minutes before they reached the attack area so as not to enable the enemy to get a 'fix' on them. The provision of these TR1143 VHF radios was soon to prove itself a vital development; the existing bomber radios, TR1196 HF R/T sets, were just not good enough for the job in hand as their objective was solely to contact the airbase; they had poor volume, suffered from extensive interference at night and became very difficult to hear over longer distances.

The TR1143 sets on the other hand had a range of up to 150 miles, though it was less than this at lower altitudes. The new role of 'master bomber' could not work unless the man in charge of the mission was in charge of everyone else and he could not be so unless he had the right equipment. That which was provided would certainly prove itself on 17 May.

Now that they could at last see their objective, Gibson thought that in the silvery moon-rays 'it looked squat and heavy and unconquerable; it looked grey and solid in the moonlight, as though it were part of the countryside itself and just as immovable'. They would soon find themselves flying direct into flak, which would shoot out at them from along the dam's walls, 'like a battleship' as they seemed to him. The absence of searchlights subdued the light but the colours of the tracer would soon be shooting up like a deadly rainbow, green, yellow and red, attempting to bring down the impudent aircraft that were invading German airspace.

For the flak gunners at the Möhne, it was difficult at first to ascertain what was about to happen. Given Gibson's dummy run and the sounds of aircraft, they knew that there were planes in the vicinity but they could not at first see them, so they fired up some shells randomly to deter any would-be attackers. Within a very short space of time, the aircraft were firing back. The gunners were soon able to pick out the planes as distant, black, menacing shadows. The job of the gunners was about to be made easier as each plane would switch on its spotlights when it moved in for its attack.

The Möhne lake is aligned east–west. There are two main arms, cut in two by a wooded peninsula with a high point, known as the Heversburg, rising to 860 feet above sea level; the surface of the lake when full lies at a point that is 700 feet above sea level. The dam lies at the north-west corner of the lake and runs along an approximate line of north-east to south-west. The line of attack required the aircraft to line up over the Hevearm (the southern arm of the lake) and then dive down over the treetops on the Heversburg peninsula, pointing like a fingerpost towards the dam wall itself, at a speed of 220 mph.

It has been calculated that reaching optimum height of 60 feet about a mile from the dam would, at the speed they were travelling, leave only 11 seconds before the dropping point was reached – not a lot of time, particularly when the aircraft were under heavy fire. There were for the attackers some pleasant surprises in store though. Bomb-aimer Edward Johnson on AJ-N was amazed that there was no night fighter cover over the dam. Gibson on the other hand thought that there were night fighters but that the planes were too low for them to be spotted.

The attack itself would be a real team effort. The wireless operator would be responsible for checking that the bomb was spinning at the required 500 rpm, while the navigator would line up the two spotlights on the water to confirm that they were at the right height. The bomb-aimer would of course be responsible for releasing the bomb from his prone position at the front of the aircraft while the pilot steered the plane. The engineer would be on hand to take over control of the plane if the pilot should be shot. He was also responsible for making sure that the plane was at the right speed as it made its approach for an attack while the gunners were waiting to see if any flak opened up – they would then return fire. The rear gunner would also be in the best position, given his vantage point, to assess the damage that the bomb had caused before anyone else as well as firing back at the anti-aircraft guns after the dam had been overflown.

The front gunner's task assumed greater importance than was normally the case at this point in an attack. The front turret was normally unmanned in the Lancaster at this stage in a raid as the chances of head-to-head confrontations with fighters was remote (the front gunner would by now usually have become the bomb-aimer in a conventional raid). However, on this occasion, with the planes flying at low level straight into flak, there was no chance of that happening. There were two .303 Browning guns at the front of the plane and four more in the rear turret. Rear-gunner Richard Trevor-Roper, who was in Gibson's AJ-G, was the squadron's gunnery leader. He had an important job to perform given the presence of flak positions around the dam. In the light of this need for guns at forward and rear, it was perhaps as well that a suggestion by a senior RAF officer made in February 1942, to get rid of the front turret in the Lancaster as it was never likely to be used in practice, was not taken up.

Now that they were all on-station, Gibson would launch the first attack while the rest of the planes hid out in the hills a few miles off, waiting for their turn. Flight Officer Johnson in AJ-N looked on. This first attack would not be altogether encouraging; those involved in or observing it were surprised at the amount of flak, which was 'rather more than anyone had anticipated'. Johnson thought that the defenders were quite heroic to carry on firing while the bombs were being dropped and he had a point – the impact of these massive bombs must have been terrifying when experienced close at hand. He and his comrades no doubt wished that the gunners' enthusiasm to fight back would diminish rather more quickly than it did.

At 0028 Gibson moved in to drop his bomb. The gunners defended the dam very aggressively. In preparation for the attack, Gibson's plane circled wide and over the hills at the eastern end of the lake. Then it dived down towards the waters now some two miles ahead. The crew would fly in over the Torhaus Bridge, behind the Heversberg. They would then have to hop up over the hill and then quickly down the other side before flying the last short leg to the dam itself.

By now they could see the silhouette of the two towers in front. The light was exceptional and they picked out virtually everything, though this was a dubious benefit as it would of course help the defenders too. And then the lights were switched on and Gibson looked for that perfect position, 60 feet above the surface. The spinning of the bomb had been started some 10 minutes beforehand. All was now ready. The attackers were about to prove that they had the guts and skill to deliver the bomb; all that remained was to see whether or not Wallis's science worked as well.

Pilot Officer Torger Taerum, Gibson's navigator, looked through the starboard blister window in the canopy behind the pilot. He was the only one who could see whether the lights were touching to form a 'figure of eight' or not, the moment at which the plane was at 60 feet, the exact altitude at which the bomb drop must take place. The bomb-aimer, 'Spam' Spafford, stared ahead at the dam and in particular at the basic bomb-aiming device that needed to line up with the towers on the dam to tell him that the dropping point had been reached.

They were able to get a good sight of the dam wall. But naturally enough, with the lights now on, the gunners could see them very well too. The tracer spat out from the anti-aircraft guns again, this time with a specific target in mind. The Lancaster moved on at a rate of four miles a minute towards the massive structure its crew wished to destroy, which paradoxically also bore the means of their own destruction: those persistent, angry anti-aircraft guns. A sense of fear pervaded the plane; even the practised nerves of Gibson were sensible to the fact that in a minute he might be dead. He told Pulford, sitting next to him, to be ready to take over control of the aircraft if he should be hit. It was a prospect, Gibson later admitted, that made him feel rather gloomy.

There was perhaps a hint of irony in this statement, later made in Gibson's book. He described his flight engineer as 'a sincere and plodding Londoner', which is a blatant error as Pulford came from Yorkshire, a part of the country whose typical accent is very hard for anyone who listens briefly to it to confuse with that of the capital. In fact, these words were toned down by the censor from the original version in which Gibson's own words described Pulford as 'a bit of a dummy'. In the event, very little was said in the cockpit of Gibson's plane; it has often been suggested that this was because of their different social backgrounds and the fact that Pulford was 'only' an NCO. This has led one biographer of Gibson to say that the atmosphere in the cockpit reflected that of a 'master and servant' relationship. Gibson allegedly also did not have a lot of time for front-gunner Deering, another NCO, either.

But at this precise moment, any personal prejudices needed to be put to one side. The moment of truth was at hand. Now 'Spam' Spafford was lining up his bomb-sight. The flak blazed on; Gibson had been through much worse but it was the lowness of the plane that preyed on the nerves; a mistake at this altitude and there would be no time to recover or bale out. He also felt that his plane was tiny compared to the vast bulk of the dam wall. But as the flak gunners continued their rapid firing, by some miracle Gibson was not hit.

Gibson was conscious of his own plane's guns spitting back at the gunners on the dam wall and the smell of burnt cordite in the cockpit as they attempted to silence the enemy and make the run-in easier for both themselves and those who were to follow. At the same time, they also had to concentrate on getting the aircraft into exactly the right position. Spafford told Gibson to make minor adjustments to left and right before, once they were in the right spot, telling him to hold the plane steady. Pulford crouched next to him, dreading the moment that he might have to take control of the plane if Gibson were hit. Almost before he knew it, they were reaching the moment of no return.

The time was now 0028. The spotlights underneath the plane had converged and the spot for releasing the bomb was rapidly approaching. Even as the flak continued to try and blow them out of the sky, Spafford released the weapon. Relieved of the 9000-lb bomb weight, the aircraft shot upwards, leaving the crew's stomachs down at water level as the plane ascended rapidly. As the plane soared up over the dam wall, rear-gunner Trevor-Roper fired at the anti-aircraft positions quickly receding in their slipstream.

Those of the crew who could see out of the plane peered into the moonlit night to see if their efforts had met with success. A red flare was fired from the plane, the pre-arranged signal to show that the bomb had been dropped. There was a massive explosion and a huge column of water spouted up towards the night sky. Even as they watched, they could see a huge plume of water 1,000 feet high still hanging in the air. Through the drizzly cloud, they could see that the surface of the water was now disturbed and turbulent, a stark contrast to the mirror-like smoothness of not long before. Water was seen rushing over the top of the dam but despite their initial optimism the wall was still as solid as ever.

Then the surface of the water calmed down, no breach in the dam wall could be seen. Investigations carried out by the German authorities after the raid suggested that the bomb may have hit the torpedo net. It may also have veered off to the left, a major risk if the plane was not exactly level when the bomb was dropped or if it were released too far back from the dam. There was also an inherent risk in the bomb itself in that during the trials the smaller Highball weapon had performed with more consistency than the Upkeep device used during the dam raids.

This lack of success was anyway not altogether surprising. Wallis had felt that several hits might be needed before the dam was breached and Gibson hoped that he had done his part in softening up the defences and paving the way for other planes to finish the job off. Now his job was to shepherd his flock through the rest of the assault until the dam was at last breached.

For the Germans, a sense of alarm was starting to hit home. The reaction of Clemens Köhler, an engineer in the power station behind the dam, was to run up the hill after telephoning a warning. This was no time to be staying down at low level in the shadow of the dam. It was clear now that it was the dam that these planes were after. He did not want to be down at low level should they succeed. The building was right underneath the dam and would be submerged in seconds should the wall give way.

Those on the dam were understandably badly shaken up by the huge explosion followed by the plume of water that resulted from the first bomb that had been dropped. The structure they were on was clearly the objective for the attackers and they were all that stood between the enemy and the massive masonry walls of the dam they were guarding. The sound of the explosion reverberated around them. As they waited to see whether or not the walls would hold, they were inundated with giant waves as high as houses battering the top of the dam wall.

On a hill above the Möhne reservoir, Max Schulze-Sölde, an artist who lived in a house near the dam, watched as a bomber flew over. He was mesmerised as it passed close by and wondered what it was there for. Soon after the plane passed, there was a huge explosion, the blast from which threw him back into his house. Getting to his feet, he looked down at the dam but saw that it was still reassuringly intact.

Soon after Gibson's bomb was dropped, the results of the first attack were Morsed back to Grantham, where Harris, Wallis and Cochrane among others were in attendance. The tension was already starting to build as everyone knew that the time for the attack on the dam 400 miles away was imminent. As this was the first time that the weapon had been used in anger, there was no certainty that it would work. The pressure on Wallis was enormous. He had argued for years that he could develop a bomb to breach the dam and now his bluff had been well and truly called.

If he was wrong, the personal humiliation would be enormous. His career could be ruined by failure and he was also very aware of the fact that men's lives would be lost because of him. Perhaps worst of all, there was the stern, searing face of Harris close by. Harris had never been convinced that the raid was going to work. His reaction should the raids not be a success did not bear thinking about.

Harris had after all been incensed that these inventors were putting the lives of his men at risk. What if Harris had been right all along and Wallis had been wrong? Lives would be lost and all for nothing. That surely was the worst thought of all.

Now, as the tension started to increase, the first message was received. It was 'Goner 58A'. This meant that the bomb had exploded between 5 and 50 yards short of its target. There was no report of any breach. Although this did not yet mean that the raid was bound to fail, it was also clearly not the initial success that everyone had hoped for. The tension went up another notch. So too did Wallis's nervousness while the granite features of Harris turned still sterner. Wallis's science remained as yet unproven and Harris's scepticism in contrast remained justified. This was going to be a long and trying night. And the news would get worse before it got better.

5

Breach of Möhne Dam: Nigger at Target X

00.31–01.00, Monday 17 May

With Gibson's bomb away and with no apparent impact on the dam, the first seeds of doubt were sown both among the aircrews above the Möhne reservoir and also those waiting for news back at Grantham. The bomb after all was experimental in design and had never been used in action before. With extreme precision required, there were tiny fractions of error involved. If the plane were not straight when the bomb was released, if it were too high or too low, if the bomb were dropped too early or too late, then there was no certainty that success would be achieved.

So many imponderables, so much that could go wrong. All of a sudden, it must have started to become apparent that this was after all in some ways still an experiment, as Wallis had said without perhaps realising the full significance of his statement. And the problem with experiments was that until they had been tried for real no one could be sure of their final conclusion.

In the meantime, those below the planes, the people who would be right in the line of the floodwaters should they be released if the bombers achieved their objective, remained oblivious to the danger they were in. Despite the fact that there were those in Germany who accepted the possibility of the dams being breached and argued that precautions should be developed to protect against such an eventuality, the authorities as a whole had remained complacent about the threat and no early-warning schemes had been developed in case the dams were breached. Hundreds of civilians would pay for that complacency with their lives.

That made it worse was that it was known by now that there were British planes in the area. It was at around 0030 that the first air-raid warning was received at Neheim, some 10 kilometres from the Möhne dam and right in the path of any floodwaters that might be released from the reservoir if the wall was breached. Leutnant Dicke, the duty officer in the police station at Neheim, had heard aircraft engines and gone out to see what was happening at around 0015. Not long after, he heard a muffled explosion. This was the first sign that something significant was starting to unfold in the region.

By now, Regierungspdirektor (Government Director) Niewisch, an important local official, had gone to Arnsberg town hall. Low-flying aircraft indicated a threat and he needed to try and establish what the raiders were trying to achieve. Clemens Köhler, the engineer from the Möhne dam, had phoned his superiors in the settlements of Niederense and Neheim, the first areas of significant population below the dams, expressing his fears should the dam be breached. However unlikely a breach might seem, no one was in any doubt as to what its consequences would be.

But the consistent feature about much of the German response to the attacks was its misplaced sense of security. The response to Köhler from the authorities at Neheim was not to worry them with fairy tales. There was a similar reaction from elsewhere, or perhaps non-reaction would be a more appropriate description. There were, for example, night fighters at the nearby base of Werl, just a few miles away (they could have been at the dam in minutes) but none of them were scrambled during the raid. The German authorities carried on in blissful ignorance of just how much danger the inhabitants of the Möhne valley and the wider Ruhr region were in.

The fear of night fighters was a real one for the raiders, but the British planes in the vicinity of the Möhne dam remained completely undisturbed. Now that he had dropped his bomb without success, Gibson had to revert to his role of master bomber. He had to wait for a few minutes after the bomb was dropped before the next attack could be launched. First of all, he needed to establish whether the wall had been breached or not. Then he had to wait for the waters to calm down after being whipped up by the massive explosion, otherwise the bomb would not run true across the surface.

After a short wait, it became apparent that there was clearly no breach. By 0033, Gibson was happy that the time was now right for the next plane to move into the attack, that of his close confidant 'Hoppy' Hopgood. Gibson signalled the code word 'Cooler 2' over the VHF radio. This was the signal for Hopgood to launch his attack, 'Cooler' being the code to do so and the '2' being the number of the plane in the flight that was assigned to Hopgood's aircraft, meaning that in the master plan he was to move in next. As Hopgood got into position, Gibson radioed across the reassuring message that 'it's a piece of cake'.

But in the event, it was anything but. The turbulence of the water had died away but the flak gunners on the dam were now fully aware of what to expect next. Gibson had enjoyed the element of surprise; Hopgood would not. Gibson watched on with concern as 'Hoppy' and his crew followed the same route in as he had a few minutes before. Anxious minutes lay ahead.

The German defenders were ready but there was a great deal of nervousness present among them now that they realised that the dam they were guarding was clearly the objective of the British bombers they could dimly see without the benefit of searchlights. Nearby, Ferdinand Nölle had now been joined, and theoretically relieved, by Wilhelm Strotkamp. Nölle warned him not to go down into the galleries built into the dam. He was afraid that he would be drowned if he did so. In the event, Nölle would not be going anywhere; he could see that he was still needed where he was.

Karl Schütte, who was in charge of the guns on Tower 1, told his men to prepare for the attack. Hopgood got into position and lined up his plane for the assault. He got his plane into exactly the right spot for the approach as far as he was able, ensured that it was at the right height and set course for the dam. Aiming for the midpoint between the two towers he ploughed on as if oblivious to the flak now directed at him. The spotlights beneath his plane were now on, lighting it up as a target for the gunners.

A screen of flak was thrown up, a seemingly impenetrable barrier through which Hopgood and his men had to pass if they wished to claim their prize. It would not be easy. Long lines of shells spat up into the sky above the calm waters of the reservoir, homing in with unerring accuracy on the cumbersome Lancaster as it trundled determinedly towards the dam walls. As Hopgood hurtled closer, Schütte saw the tracer clearly hit the plane. Then a flame billowed out. Exhilarated, Schütte shouted out, 'It's burning! It's burning!' He later recalled that 'a great cheer went up, just like when you've scored'.

But the exultation was short-lived, for a massive explosion soon followed, with stones flying everywhere and the gunners on the dam being thrown to the ground. When the defenders looked behind them, the power station that had once stood at the base of the massive edifice was nowhere to be seen; all that remained was a pile of smoking rubble. To the north-west, a more distant explosion told of a crashed aircraft.

All this appeared to happen in seconds, but for those involved it seemed a lifetime. The artist Max Schulze-Sölde, now wide awake, had been looking on as Hopgood approached the dam. Even as he watched the plane disappear over the hills to be followed by a violent cacophony as it crashed, the power station went up in front of him. Wilhelm Strotkamp was much closer to the action; he was on watch at the dam. When he saw the planes beginning their attack, he ran for shelter in a tunnel under the dam wall, just about the worse place he could have gone as it happened.

What had actually happened in these few dramatic minutes was this. As Hopgood had been aiming his plane like an arrow for the heart of the dam, the tracer had started to hit home. Both port engines had been hit and all power to the rear turret had been lost. Then the tracer had seriously damaged the starboard wing and a fire also broke out in one of the starboard engines. These were, taken together, devastating blows and left the plane with little chance of survival, especially as it may have been damaged by flak earlier on in the raid.

But the plane had still ploughed on despite the hits that had been suffered. Now they were close to the dam wall. At this moment bomb-aimer Jim Fraser released the bomb. It was past the point at which he should have done so but it is not clear whether the late release was because of an error on Fraser's part or because he already realised that the plane was in serious trouble and the last thing they wanted was over 6,000 lb of explosive left on board should the plane crash. Better anyway to cause some damage to the dam than none at all. Dropping the bomb in the right place now anyway became an irrelevance because it was obvious that the plane would not be up to making another run in to get in the right place. It was now a question of survival for those on board.

As the bomb had been dropped later than it should have been, it bounced right over the wall (which was fairly low above the surface of the lake given the high levels of the water in the reservoir) and down into the power station that was behind it. A massive explosion followed that created chaos in the building. Fortunately for Wilhelm Strotkamp he had realised the error of his ways and had already started to make his way up the hill. As the power station blew up, great chunks of masonry showered down around him. Given the proximity of the bomb strike and the large mass of explosive that the weapon had been carrying, he was very lucky to survive.

In his position in the nose of the plane as it staggered along, Fraser had been conscious of a tremendous crash on board the aircraft and a fire then breaking out. It was initially extinguished but then took hold again. As Hopgood struggled to gain height and fly over the hills behind the dam, the gunners on the wall could see the plane aflame.

Minchin, Hopgood's wireless operator, mortally wounded and with his leg virtually severed, still managed to fire off the Very light to confirm that the bomb been released which showed an incredible sense of duty and clear thinking given the state that he was in. The plane was now doomed. The fire in the starboard engine could not be extinguished and all that remained was to bale out. This was particularly difficult for Burcher who had to crank his rear turret back into position by hand as hydraulic power was no longer available to do it automatically. He needed to get back into the plane to get his parachute on as it could not be worn in the rear turret due to lack of space.

The recommended escape route would then be to get back into the rear turret and get out through there after cranking it round but that would take too long as the plane, even after attempting to gain height, was only a few hundred feet off the ground and could crash into it within seconds. Therefore he decided to take the only other practical way out; through the starboard side entry door.

Burcher cranked his turret around as quickly as possible to reach his parachute back in the main fuselage. Despite the extreme seriousness of the situation, discipline and training kicked in; he got to the intercom and told Hopgood he was about to jump – 'Get out, you bloody fool!' came the reply. Hopgood's last words were, 'If only I had another 300 feet – I can't get any more height.'

As he did this, a terrible sight met him. His friend John Minchin had managed to drag himself over the main spar and into the main fuselage. With his leg hanging off and having to be dragged along behind him when he did this, the strength of will required to perform this act despite the agonising pain he must have been in can only be imagined. Burcher put a parachute on Minchin before pushing him through the door, holding on to the ripcord to ensure that it opened once Minchin was out of the plane. Sadly, his heroism was in vain as Minchin would not survive his terrible injuries.

Having done his own heroic part in trying to save Minchin, Burcher could now worry about himself. It is not clear whether Burcher jumped out of the plane or was blown out by an explosion but in any event he managed to bale out. In fact, he was unconscious during the climactic following moments. His parachute failed to deploy fully but did so enough to slow down his descent sufficiently for him to survive. When he came to, he was lying on the ground. On the short journey down, he had clipped the tail-plane and broken his back. He now lay there helpless and all he could do was wait until he was captured.

Burcher's terror was not yet over, for he could not be sure that, if the dam were breached, he would not be in the line of the floods with no possibility of moving himself out of their path. But he would in the event survive and be taken into captivity, where he would be harshly cross-examined and lose several teeth in the process; he was later interred in Stalag Luft III, famous as being the setting for the 'Great Escape', where he managed to obtain some false teeth made of toilet porcelain.

Pilot Officer J. W. Fraser, a Canadian, was the only other survivor. He had unpacked his parachute as quickly as possible inside the confined space at the front of the stricken Lancaster but was horrified when he opened the hatch in the floor to see how close the treetops were. If his parachute did not open instantly he was doomed. He fell from, rather than jumped out of, the plane and his 'chute was barely opened before he hit the ground with a thud. He had witnessed the tail-wheel whistle past him as he was in the air.

Nearby, Gibson had been watching on horrified as the action unfolded. He was able to see Hopgood's plane with one of the fuel tanks ablaze. Then the plane had exploded. He had witnessed Hopgood's attempts to gain height and then at an altitude of about 500 feet saw an explosion lighting up the sky and a wing blown off. The rest of the plane disintegrated and fell to the ground, still burning like stars that had fallen from the sky.

Hopgood's plane crashed into the ground a few miles north of the Möhne dam, near the village of Ostönnen on the road between Soest and Werl. It came to rest in a farmer's field, an unremarkable and mundane place to meet a hero's end. Today a small plaque still marks the spot, not far from where motorway traffic hurries past, oblivious to the drama that was played out nearby.

Five men had lost their lives and Burcher lay incapacitated on the ground. However, one man from Hopgood's plane still had an opportunity to escape. John Fraser's war was not yet over. He managed to run off after landing in a cornfield. Miraculously he had barely a scratch on him. He would stay a free man for ten days, heading for the Netherlands and living off potatoes and turnips. However, he was then captured and also sent to Stalag Luft III, where he would actually play a part in the renowned 'Great Escape'. Having been married for just seventeen days when the raid took place, Fraser returned home unannounced after the war ended. His wife Doris fainted when she saw him. It was tragically ironic that he would die in 1962 in a plane crash.

Fraser would be thoroughly interrogated before being sent off into captivity. A full report of the interrogation was sent to Hermann Goering, dated 19 June 1943. It suggests that Fraser handed over a lot of information, perhaps under some duress. However, it is not clear how honest Fraser was being, as he suggested that the bomb was spinning at 380 revolutions per minute though he had earlier on suggested it had been 400–500 (it was of course 500 and perhaps Fraser was being deliberately evasive).

He also told the Germans that the release point was 900 feet from the dam wall when in fact it was 450 yards, or 1,350 feet – as a bomb-aimer Fraser was probably very well acquainted with the exact distances involved. He further said that he could not give any information about where the final practice runs were held. He also gave the airspeed at release as 260 mph, which was too fast though he did give the correct height at which the bomb should be dropped: 60 feet. He said to his interrogator that Maudslay's bomb-aimer was Flying Officer Tytherleigh, which was also incorrect: he was his front gunner. The interrogating officer noted that 'F is very proud of his involvement in the raid on the dams' and it is not hard to imagine him playing a dangerous little game with his inquisitors by giving them information that was wrong but no so wrong as to be transparently ridiculous.

Fraser and Burcher's interrogation after their capture was a routine activity when aircrew were captured. The Germans built up substantial files on RAF activities and personnel (this was one reason, perhaps the main one, why Harris did not want his senior commanders accompanying their men on missions). As Burcher's experience shows, the interrogators were not afraid to dispense with niceties in the quest for valuable information. Although three men would survive their aircraft crashing that night and be taken into captivity, their ordeal was far from over.

But proper respect was at least shown to those who lost their lives. The bodies of the five dead airmen from the remains of Hopgood's shattered aircraft (which was almost completely obliterated in the crash) were later recovered and buried with full military honours at 1130 on 20 May at a cemetery in Soest. Their remains were ultimately exhumed and reburied at a military cemetery at Rheinberg on 14 August 1947.

Gibson also witnessed the explosion caused by Hopgood's bomb. Even as Gibson and his crew watched the last moments of 'Hoppy' and AJ-M, there was a massive blast from down below. It went up behind the power station with a tremendous explosion, which was followed by a large pall of smoke hanging in the air over it. This obscured visibility and meant that time would be needed to let the smoke clear before another attack could be made on the still intact dam. It was interesting that Gibson's account suggests that the bomb exploded after Hopgood crashed; presumably the 90-second self-destruct mechanism was working.

Hopgood was just twenty-two years old when he died but was already something of a veteran. He had previously been with 106 Squadron, regarded as one of 5 Group's best. He had flown his first two Lancaster sorties in thousand-bomber raids over Cologne and Essen in May 1942 and had completed forty-six missions with 106 Squadron and been awarded the DFC when he transferred to Syerston, where he test-piloted the new Mark II Lancaster. He had been awarded a Bar to his DFC and officially joined the newly formed 617 Squadron on 30 March 1943.

He became a very close colleague of Gibson, who would feel his loss keenly. But he would not be forgotten. John Fraser returned to Canada after the war and named his son John Hopgood Fraser after the man who had given him the opportunity to save his own life. Hopgood's valiant last efforts had after all not been in vain.

Despite the early release of the weapon from Hopgood's plane, the blast had, however, made an important contribution which would help the other planes that still had to make their attack. The gun posted on the left-hand sluice tower was blown from its footings in the explosion that demolished the power station and was rendered useless. The crew of the now redundant flak position ran along the still undamaged top of the wall to help the crew of the right-hand tower gun with the movement of ammunition. The blast had also knocked out electricity in the valley below the power station.

While the rest of Gibson's flight waited their turn to attack the dam, the first plane to arrive back in England, that of Les Munro, was landing at Scampton at 0036. With his radio out of action, he could not communicate with the control tower and therefore had to use his own initiative to land. This came as something of a surprise to those waiting back at base for whom the time was passing dreadfully slowly.

Adjutant Humphries had been spending the time talking to a WAAF, Second Officer Fay Gillon. The men liked having her around. She was pretty and Humphries later noted that such qualities, despite popular perceptions about glamorous WAAFs, were in short supply. Then they heard the unexpected drone of an aircraft overhead: it was Munro returning. Seeing that his bomb was still attached, they knew that his raid had been unsuccessful. Munro was understandably furious that he had been unable to complete his mission. Munro and later Rice, who arrived back at 0047, joined those waiting anxiously for news of the rest of the squadron. They and their crews would at least live to fight another day.

For Rice in particular the return trip had been a nerve-wracking one due to the damage done to his plane and he was forced to circle around Scampton for 20 minutes while some of the crew hand-cranked the wheels down. Then, just as he was about to land, Munro – who was of course unable to communicate with anyone given his damaged radio equipment – had cut across in front of him, delaying Rice's landing. Without a tail-wheel, which had been damaged in the close encounter with the ocean, it was also a bumpy landing and more damage was done to the plane.

Back at the Möhne, the next plane now prepared to make its run on the dam. Gibson must have been distressed by the loss of Hopgood but as a consummate professional kept his emotions in check. The crews yet to make a run now had to cope not only with the flak they knew was waiting to give them a warm reception, but also the far from welcome sight of the wreckage of Hopgood's plane burning in the hills in the near distance, a disturbing reminder of their own mortality and the risks that they were about to take.

Gibson was also of course aware that two bombs had now been dropped and the dam remained stubbornly intact. Although he would have realised that Hopgood's bomb had overshot the dam, the fact that the huge explosion had left the vast bulk of the structure unmoved ratcheted up the tension another notch.

It was Mick Martin who had the unenviable task of being next in line. At 0038 he moved in for the third attack on the Möhne dam with the moon shining on his port beam. The flak was still strong despite being one gun down by now. In order to help Martin, Gibson was flying close by, trying to give support and distract fire. However, Martin's run was not helped by the fact that there was still smoke over the target from the last attack by Hopgood.

On the dam wall, Karl Schütte and his comrades prepared to repulse the next assault. Buoyed by their success in bringing down Hopgood, they were determined to play their part in beating off the raid. At first they were distracted by Gibson's plane on the wing, but then Martin dropped down and headed straight for the wall. The flak gunners once more homed in on the plane and, according to Schütte, 'again the shells whipped towards the attacker and several hits were scored'.

But the plane spat back at the flak guns, the tracer 'like a string of pearls, the luminous spur of the shells came towards the tower like large glow-worms', as Schütte put it. The special night tracer lit up the moonlit sky as it spat out towards the defenders of the dam; it was so dazzling that a number of pilots expressed dissatisfaction with it after the raid and it was one part of the mission which seems to have divided opinion as to how efficacious it was. Inexorably, Martin and AJ-P moved in on the dam. When bomb-aimer Bob Hay thought they were in the right spot, he released the weapon.

They waited to see what impact their weapon would have. However, it did not find its target. A German report after the raid noted that the bomb did not hit the wall but exploded near the bank about 100 metres from it – British accounts record it as 20 yards short. The swell from the blast caused water to spill over the top but there was little damage to the nearby inn other than some windows blown in as a result of the blast. The starboard outer fuel tank and ailerons of AJ-P were damaged by cannon fire, but Martin managed to return safely to base despite the fact that he lost all the petrol from one of his wing-tanks.

So that was now three bombs away and still no sign of a breach. The huge plume of water when the bomb was dropped obscured the view of Martin's observer, the rear gunner Flight Sergeant Simpson, who was trying to watch how many times that the bomb bounced but could not see. Wallis was aware that the cylindrical shape of the bomb made it vulnerable to going off course if it hit the surface at the wrong angle and possibly the bomb had been dropped when the plane was not quite 'flat' in the air, causing the weapon to veer off.

It may be significant too that Martin's plane was carrying the bomb accidentally dropped on the hard standing at Scampton that morning and that might have affected the trueness of its course. However, he might also have banked slightly at the last moment to get the right bearing. In any event, the bomb veered into a narrow inlet and exploded without any real effect.

But the attacks were also taking a toll on the flak gunners. The barrels of their guns were overheating because of the fierce fire they were directing at the planes swooping down on them; but the barrels were swapped and the weapons were oiled. The attackers were of course unaware of these problems and there were now concerns expressed among the British crews that the dam was still apparently as strong as ever; Dave Shannon later said that there was some disappointment at this stage that the dam had not yet been breached, which must rank as something of an understatement.

It was now the turn of 'Dinghy' Young to take his run at the dam. Gibson warned Young to beware of the flak, which was very hot. He moved his plane to the other side of the dam in a successful attempt to distract the gunners' attention – he even switched his identification lights on so that they would divert the attention of the gunners onto his plane, hoping to give Young a clearer run in as a result.

Young went through a similar routine to the other pilots as he prepared his run in. Martin was now flying on one side of Young while Gibson flew over the wall with his lights on to confuse and draw the fire of the defenders. As the moon shone down from behind the aircraft (several pilots remarked that it would have been better ahead of rather than behind them) Young flew low over the water, his front gunner Gordon Yeo exchanging gunfire with the flak gunners, who were sticking manfully to their task. In what appeared to be exactly the right spot, bomb-aimer Vincent MacCausland released the weapon at 0043. It skimmed across the surface of the water and bounced into the dam wall. There was an almighty explosion and a massive plume of water that shot up hundreds of feet.

Young was euphoric. Everything seemed to have gone like clockwork. He could not yet see through the misty veil of the water that was showering back down over the dam walls. He could not assess with certainty whether the dam had been breached or not but he was certain that it had. Gibson though, closely watching on from AJ-G, believed that it was not and that it would take at least one more attack. It was Gibson who was right. Code 78A was Morsed back to Grantham – 'bomb despatched and hit wall but no breach observed'.

No doubt the wording of Operation Chastise's operation order now started to hit home: 'Destruction of the dam may take some time to become apparent, and careful reconnaissance may be necessary to distinguish between breaching of the dam and the spilling over the top which will follow each explosion.' Plenty of water had been seen spouting up into the air and over the dam wall but there was still no breach apparent. Young's attack appeared to be textbook and the question that was now being asked by virtually everyone in Gibson's flight was whether the plan would work at all.

There was nothing for Gibson to do but be persistent and continue to send his men into the assault and continue to hammer away at the dam. At 0048 David Maltby was given the OK by Gibson to begin his run. His navigator Vivian Nicholson noted 'flak none too light'. This time Gibson would fly off his right wing and Martin on his left.

By 0049 Maltby was moving in for his attack. The luck of the British pilots was about to change. Just now the AA gun fired by Schütte had jammed after a premature explosion in the barrel. His crew tried to clear it away with a hammer and a metal spike but to no avail. While one other gun was still active, the other men left could only fire back with basic weapons now. During the fifth attack, some of the defenders therefore used their carbines. Now that the defenders had only one gun left, the attacking planes had things pretty much to themselves. And even this last flicker of resistance was soon extinguished by gunfire from the planes.

Maltby was now charging over the surface of the water towards the dam. As he got closer, he was all of a sudden certain that he could see a minor breach in the dam. There was debris on the crest of the dam and he thought he could also see a small hole in its structure. Again his approach was textbook, though he turned slightly to port when he saw what he thought was a breach in the wall already. The bomb was released at what his bomb-aimer, John Fort, believed to be exactly the right spot. It hit the water and spun across it, bouncing true and straight. Like a dart it headed for the massive fortress-like walls of the dam in their path. The bomb hit home and a huge explosion reverberated around the shores of the reservoir.

The British pilots looked on with baited breath. But then, more disappointment. Maltby stared down through a plume of water that he estimated to be 1,000 feet high silhouetted against the moon, but as it started to settle he could see no breach in the wall and another '78A' message was sent. Neither could Gibson see anything because of the smoke and the water plumes, so Dave Shannon was ordered up to go next.

Schütte and his comrades were now virtually powerless to resist, but they had continued to look on as if they could bring down by willpower alone the attacking aircraft piloted by Maltby. Schütte had stood defiantly on his tower, with the lake in front of him, the valley behind, and under attack from all directions. It was, according to him, now child's play for the pilot whose outline he could almost see in the cockpit of the aircraft. As the bomb dropped, the lake quivered once more and a giant wave developed.

Ferdinand Nölle had stubbornly stuck around to see how the raid developed and had been going through a harrowing experience as a result. He recalled that 'each explosion in the lake was followed by a massive blast. Once I shot three metres across the duty room and bashed my head against a door. It was a good job I was wearing a steel helmet otherwise I'd have my head smashed in. This explosion was worse than anything I'd experienced at Verdun. Strotkamp arrived in the duty room out of breath from below the dam where I'd been on duty. All the windows had been blown out of the duty room and the lights had gone out.'

Like Gibson and Maltby, Schütte too waited to see what would happen to the dam wall. Of course, being closer to the action than any of the attackers he was quite possibly the first to see for sure what the effect of the bomb had been. As visibility improved, Schütte looked at the dam and saw, perhaps before anyone else, that it was breached. Even as he watched, the water poured through the hole in its centre which was getting visibly bigger by the second. There was now no doubt about it – the dam had gone.

Wilhelm Strotkamp had been making his way up the hill towards safety and had sheltered behind a tree when he heard another explosion, but this one was ominously different than the ones he had heard previously. As he watched he saw that the dam wall appeared to be trembling, almost as if it were a living being. Then to his horror and disbelief he had seen the wall start to split. Then the cracks began to widen and, before he could make sense of it all, what had been a small gap looked as if it were a barn door being opened.

Ferdinand Nölle was increasingly horrified by what he saw. Then a phone rang, which he answered. It was the authorities in Soest asking what was going on. He told them about the breach and suggested that they warn those in the valley; there was nothing more he could do. Soest and its immediate environs would be safe due to its location but for those living in the Möhne valley a terrifying night was unfolding. The only hope was to arrange an evacuation of the narrow and confined valley as quickly as possible. But for many it was already too late. Nölle looked back below the dam but he could see nothing save a fog of spray from the water that was now pouring through the breach.

The boys on the northern lakeshore at Delecke could not see the dam itself but they could work out what was happening to some extent from the noise and also from observing the planes in the early part of their run. Walter Fischer and his mates had watched as

again and again the bombers flew at the dam wall, blazing away with all guns and churning up great streaks of vapour which were drawn along behind them. Then behind the spit of land brilliant white plumes of water shot straight up into the air followed shortly afterwards by an explosion. The fifth time there was a muffled thundering explosion. We all thought the dam had been hit.

We ran over there from Delecke [a couple of miles down the road and fortunately for them above the dam] as fast as we could. A hole had been torn in the crest of the dam and you could easily have put a block of flats into it. The water from the Möhne flowed quietly through the breach, but down in the valley it thundered up. The crashing of the water caused the roadway along the top of the dam to vibrate. I thought back to the song that we'd been listening to on our beds in the rowing club when the whole gruesome business began. There's a line in *Lili Marlene* about the whirling fog. But now a fog of doom had descended over the places in the valley which had been hit by the disaster.

There was remarkable confirmation of the more or less exact time that the dam was breached. The Institut für Geophysik at Göttingen was about 120 kilometres to the north of the Möhne. The Institut had a seismograph that was sensitive enough to pick up the shockwaves from the bombs exploding under the surface at the dam. This timed the decisive explosion at the Möhne at 0049 and 40.5 seconds which, given a time lag of around 20 seconds due to the distance that the Institut was from the dam, allows an exact time for the decisive strike to be established.

As the breach became obvious to those on the wall, so too did it become clear to the attackers. Gibson was just getting ready to coordinate Shannon's attack when a voice from elsewhere in the plane suddenly shouted, 'I think she has gone!'

Shannon was about to start out on his run when Gibson told him to hold off while he went to have a closer look at the situation. He too could see without a doubt that the dam was breached. He believed that the breach was about 150 feet in extent. He thought that the water pouring through was like 'stirred porridge'.

Others too could see the situation rapidly unfolding. The injured Burcher watched on from the hills, afraid that he would be overwhelmed by the flood while Schütte looked on helplessly as the water cascaded down the valley. From above, pilots could see headlights extinguished as the water rolled over vehicles trapped in its path. 'I saw their headlights burning and I saw water overtake them, wave by wave, and then the colour of the headlights underneath the water changing from light blue to green, from green to dark purple, until there was no longer anything except the water bouncing down in great waves,' Gibson said as the horror that he and his men had unleashed started to overwhelm the land below the dam.

This was not the only action going on at around this time. Just a few minutes before, a very different scene had been played out at the Sorpe dam. For half an hour now McCarthy had been flying up and down trying to get the right run in to it. He also waited in vain for other planes to join him. In fact, the scene at the Sorpe could not be more different than that at the Möhne. There were no defences and the world was sleeping. McCarthy had the skies to himself.

As well as the difficult approach to the attack, McCarthy was also handicapped because the mist that had developed over the water made it hard to see clearly. Only on the tenth approach was his bomb-aimer George Johnson happy to let the bomb go. The plan was to crack the centre of the dam and start a leak. Therefore, it might be some time before the dam collapsed rather than the instantaneous impact witnessed at the Möhne.

But the frequently aborted approaches had tested the nerves of those on board the plane to breaking point. Rear gunner Dave Rodger, who was taking the full brunt of the G-force as the plane banked away on a number of occasions, was getting increasingly fed up with these repeatedly aborted attacks and felt like throwing Johnson out of the plane. They did not have the spotlights fitted on the plane so they had to guess at the height of the bomb-drop. They were going at a speed of 170 mph when the bomb was finally released.

As the bomb was dropped and they banked away, Rodger saw a huge waterspout shoot up which almost drenched him in the rear turret. Wallis, according to Johnson, had said that six hits would be needed to breach the Sorpe, but there would not be six bombs available to drop on it that night. In the excitement of at last releasing the bomb, though, something went wrong; McCarthy and his wireless operator Leonard Eaton forgot to report the drop back to Grantham until 0300.

Josef Kesting, the machinist from the power station at the Sorpe dam, witnessed this attack. He saw the plane drop something that looked like a 'huge septic tank' from its fuselage. An enormous explosion followed along with a plume of water 100 metres high. Kesting promised himself that he would come back with a basket in the morning and pick up any dead fish that he could find. He did not realise that it was the dam that was the target and assumed that the plane was after the power station.

Although McCarthy and his crew had stuck to their task admirably, they had not succeeded in breaching the dam, though they had crumbled its crest. But despite subsequent beliefs that the damage had caused the reservoir to be drained so that the walls could be properly repaired, it appears that in reality no such inconvenience was caused. The earthen core of the dam wall was simply too robust to be breached in the way envisaged. In the words of Len Sumpter, who did not admittedly witness the attack personally, 'the Sorpe was a waste of time with this bomb'.

There was nothing more for McCarthy now to do except guide his men home safely. So they now set their course back towards Scampton. Because they did not have a compass deviation card loaded for their Upkeep-less state, it was hard to navigate the prescribed return route so they just returned the way they had come. With their mission accomplished as far as they were able, their duty now was to survive.

Just a few miles off at the Möhne a scene of chaos was unfolding. At 0050 a call was logged to Leutnant Dicke at Neheim, telling him that the dam had been hit and flooding had started. It would only be a few minutes before the waters were approaching the town. Dicke passed this terrifying information onto the mayor and sent one of his men to meet him. However, by the time that he arrived the mayor's house was already partly underwater. Dicke then despatched officers to the more vulnerable parts of the town, some of which was fortunately positioned above the flood. However, a floodtide of 39 feet, moving at 13 mph, was on its way towards Neheim. By 0100 the town's telephone system was out of action and the town was essentially at the mercy of the inundation that was descending on it.

Frau Noller lived not far below the Möhne dam. When she heard the planes going over, she had hurried off to the air-raid shelters. She heard a bomber going over, almost skimming the roof of her house as it was so low. A deafening cacophony followed, as plane engines soared low overhead while the guns spat out at them. Even before the breach, the huge plumes of water spiralling up into the sky as the bombs exploded sent water pouring over the parapet of the dam. She managed to get up out of the cellars and to safety before the floods came and inundated her house.

The news of the breach of the Möhne dam had not yet been received at Grantham. As far as they were all aware, the ultimate conclusion of the raid was still very uncertain. At 0050 Young's signal arrived stating that the dam had not been breached ('Goner 78A'). As Young was flying in a different order to that planned, this suggested to those at Grantham that the attack had failed. Wallis buried his head in his hands despairingly. 'No, it's no good,' was all he could find to say. He was desperate at what he believed to be the failure of the attack. He had already seen Harris and Cochrane 'looking suspiciously at me' and even he was beginning to have doubts.

Wallis later wrote to Cochrane that 'the tense moments in the Operation Room when, after four attacks, I felt that I had failed to make good, were almost more than I could bear'. With Harris in close proximity, the tension was terrible as Wallis's plan appeared to all of those gathered around expectantly to be close to failure.

The mood was about to change completely even as Maltby and

Martin, who had dropped their bombs, were ordered home at 0053. Three minutes later, another message came across the ether to Grantham. Wing Commander Dunn, Chief Signals Officer of 5 Group, was waiting attentively to take down any messages that came in. Two, to confirm that the bombs had been released but had not breached the walls, were received from Young and Martin's aircraft at 0050 and 0053 respectively. At 0056 Dunn started to take down another Morse message. He had only taken down the three letters 'NIG' before he ran into the main ops room with the news that the dam had been breached.

With the tension now pierced, pandemonium broke out. An unusually happy Harris made his way over to Wallis and told him, 'Wallis, I didn't believe a word you said when you came to see me. But now you could sell me a pink elephant.' It was not long before the news would be telephoned over to the White House in Washington by Harris, where Churchill and his staff were visiting Roosevelt. A nice legend would develop that when Harris tried to phone the White House, he was accidentally put through to a local pub of the same name instead. Sadly there is no evidence to support this rather pleasant fiction.

Then, as an afterthought, Dunn realised that he should ask Gibson to confirm the message. One wonders what the reaction would have been should Dunn have got the wrong end of the stick and relayed an inaccurate message. At 0057 Gibson was contacted by Dunn to confirm the 'Nigger' signal, which he did with a single word answer to the enquiry – 'correct'. One single word but the import of it was immense.

Back over the Möhne, Gibson curbed the excited radio chatter that had started after the dam was burst and ordered the first wave to move off towards the Eder dam. As he, accompanied by Young and the remaining planes that had not yet dropped their bombs, headed south-east they could already see the Möhne dam emptying. There were little towns beneath them as they flew – Gibson called them 'the Baths and Exeters of Germany'. The choice of these towns in his description was perhaps deliberate, for in the so-called Baedeker raids the Germans had been targeting towns of cultural rather than industrial significance to retaliate for damage done to German cultural sites.

Now survival on the ground below the breached dam was a lottery. It depended on where you were in the valley beneath it. Günne suffered some damage but escaped obliteration, being mostly on higher ground. That said, on this particular night everything was relative. Günne was the first to be hit, within just a minute of the dam being breached at 0050. The rifle club and three power stations in the village were the first to be overwhelmed and thirty people died.

Survival was largely a matter of luck and also keeping your nerve under enormous stress. The waves were up to 8 metres high. In the inn, Adolf Nölle had the presence of mind to guide his family from out of the cellar, where they would have all died, upstairs into the loft, where they sheltered behind a chimney breast. They survived, as did the wall clock in the bar which was later recovered. However, it did not work properly and, regardless of how many times it was repaired, it always stopped at 0050.

The police and flak detachment at the Möhne dam suffered no losses at all which, given their proximity to such massive explosions, was little short of miraculous.Others though were not so lucky. As a man-made tsunami started to flow, it brought terror in its wake. Now there were only minutes for thousands to make decisions that would affect the rest of their lives. For many of them, indeed, they were decisions of life or death.

6

Devastation in Möhne Valley: Bombers Move on to Target Y

01.01–01.45, Monday 17 May

For years and decades, the sturdy walls of the Möhne dam had held back the accumulated rainwater that had showered down onto the hills, and it had collected the individually insignificant flow of the streams that would otherwise have carried on, almost unnoticed, down to the lands below. Trickle by trickle, shower by shower, stream by stream, the waters had been trapped until they formed a mighty man-made sea, from which flowed the lifeblood of the Ruhr industries. Now, with the walls shattered, the accumulated strength and power of the waters was released, unfettered and unstoppable, down onto the sleeping villages and towns that sheltered in the shadow of the dam. All that could stop the flood was its own exhaustion, when its momentum expired of its own volition. And that would not happen for many hours and many miles.

Survival depended significantly on where people lived. The village of Günne was right underneath the dam, a drop of many feet below where the dam walls stood. There was a compensating basin below the dam, which caressed the shores by the village, and then the River Möhne flowed down a valley into the Ruhr region. Günne was built partly up a hillside; those higher up the hill would be safe from the flood. Those by the shoreline were doomed, with just seconds' warning before the waters consumed their houses along with the three hydroelectric power stations on the banks of the waters.

Beyond Günne the valley then dropped, enclosed on either side by hills that would stop the waters from widening out and losing their power. Instead the deluge would be channelled into a fairly narrow area, where its force would build up with nowhere to go except on, forward, smashing everything in its way. Again those in the trough of the valley were often doomed; they had a couple of minutes' warning at most in which they could attempt to scramble uphill to safety, provided they knew that the waters were coming, which in many cases they did not.

For those down below, moments of blind terror were at hand. Just before one o'clock, the residents of Himmelpforten Farm were awoken by a tenant shouting for them to run, for the water was coming. They ran as fast as they could along a road up into some woods. The water threatened to overwhelm them as it overtook them and some were grasped by the waters and swept to their deaths. Others, luckier, managed to escape but watched in horror as the waters submerged houses and churches in their path.

A local farm worker named Kersten had also run and given the alarm as the waters approached Niederense close by to Himmelpforten. 'Save yourselves, the water is coming,' he shouted, urging others to follow him to the high ground and safety. He ran to the road with a friend, Frau Scheven. They ran towards the woods, hoping to find some kind of refuge there. Sadly, both Frau Scheven and a visiting friend and her three-year-old son were unable to outrun the torrent.

Fraulein Muller, who owned a chicken farm nearby, saw the farmhouse and vicarage at Himmelpforten fall victim to the waters. The church and its tower stood defiant for 15 minutes before they too collapsed into the flood. As day broke a few hours later, a terrible sight greeted the eyes of the traumatised survivors. Everywhere floated the corpses of livestock – cattle, hens, pigs – as well as people. An eighty-three-year-old woman had tied herself to a chimney and clung on there for grim life. She would be there for two days until she was rescued.

With the restraining wall of the dam gone, the deluge continued to pour down on the often unsuspecting inhabitants of the towns and villages below the dam. The residents of Niederense were in particular danger, being so close to the dam and with little chance of warning reaching them (though fortunately there were steep hills nearby where a number of people lived). One of those living further down was Elisabeth Hennecke, who had hidden in the cellars when she heard the air-raid alarm go some time before. Elisabeth was in a very positive frame of mind, having been earlier in the evening to the Apollo cinema in Neheim, a few miles down the valley, where she had seen a film called *Die goldene Stadt* (*The Golden City*). She had not been home long when the alarm went.

The people in the shelter were, however, uncertain as to what exactly was going on. After a while, curiosity kicked in and Elisabeth had gone outside with others to have a look. While they were there, they heard a heavy blast. Returning to the cellar, they found that there was no light: the noise they had heard had occurred when Hopgood's bomb had taken out the power station. A little while after this, the residents heard 'an ear-splitting roaring, cracking and crashing'. They went outside soon after, to find that the yard was already knee-deep in water. They rushed back in to the cellar to fetch out the elderly and children who were still there when the roof caved in.

Running upstairs, they found a ladder which they used to make their way up into the attic. From there, they climbed onto the roof to escape the rising waters. They signalled out with their pocket torches to those who had escaped to the surrounding hills. They were among the lucky ones. About six hours later they were finally rescued, to be greeted with dry clothes and warm drinks.

While on the roof, they witnessed some harrowing and terrible sights:

> With the children in front of me I sat on the ridge of the roof; I had one leg over one side and the other leg over the other ... All the joints in the house were groaning and creaking and it was rocking from side to side. Tree trunks were crashing through the half-timbered sides of the house. I just clung desperately to the roof hoping that if it gave way I'd be able to swim off with the children. The lightning conductor had got stretched out from all the pulling. The water carried a little timber-framed house past us towards Neheim and in a window on a table in one of the rooms there was a candle giving off a peculiar kind of light. Tree trunks from the saw-mill kept crashing

down in front of the house; dead cows were carried along past the roof.

It was a scene from a nightmare set in a valley of normally idyllic beauty. It changed the lives of those who lived through these terrible events. Given her experiences, it was understandable that Elisabeth later said that 'I wouldn't want to live in a valley below a dam any more. I can't escape the fear; it's always with me. I wouldn't want to go through that again.'

Another who witnessed the deluge that hit Niederense and the nearby tiny hamlet of Himmelpforten was Karl-Heinz Dohle, who had been watching the raid unfold with his father from their garden. They could clearly see the 'birds of death' and the tracer streaking across the sky. They heard explosions and then a rumbling sound.

Just before Niederense was a marvellous building, the Porta Coeli convent. It was in a wonderful, peaceful location, beside the normally placid River Möhne which day by day made its way lethargically down the narrow valley. It was a beautiful spot in an out of the way place, which hinted at its Cistercian origins. Seven hundred years before, the 'white monks' who loved places of solitude and grandeur had built a sturdy church here. Over the centuries it had accumulated some glorious art to beautify it until it was a very different building to the one it had started life as.

Now this place of solitude and contemplation became the home of terror and death. Hemmed in by the hills on either side, the waters crashed into the buildings. Dohle felt impelled to climb a hill from which he and his father saw the Porta Coeli convent inundated. For a few minutes the spire stood defiantly above the waters. Then it leaned over and plummeted into the swollen river. As it did so, Dohle could hear one last muffled clang of the bell, a final knell for the wonderful church which stood at the head of what would become known as 'Todestal' – 'Death Valley'.

Another youth, sixteen-year-old Werner Hellmann, watched on in horror from 200 metres away as the waters inundated the convent. He later recalled that 'I could clearly see the weathervane on top of the steeple sticking out of that thundering flood which by then had reached its highest point. After a while the steeple tipped over to one side and went under. The bell gave a single, dull clang.' It was a simple, solemn knell for those who were about to die.

Some of those in the path of the flood were saved by the heroism and self-sacrifice of others. One of them, Pastor Berkenkopf, the local priest, rang the bell of the convent to warn others; he gave his life to save his flock. Strangely, the Pastor seemed to have predicted his imminent death in his last sermon on Sunday 16 May when he spoke on the subject, 'In a short while you will see me no more, for I am going to the father'.

Berkenkopf was later found in the cellar seeking shelter along with others (which must call into some question whether it was him ringing the bell at all; an air-raid shelter was a strange place to run to if a flood could be seen approaching). Later, after the deluge, the local Hitler Youth were given the task of digging bodies out of the rubble (the church had been totally swallowed by the waters). They eventually dug their way into the cellar and found the pastor's body. It was reverently taken away on a stretcher for a Christian burial.

Then daylight came a few hours later it brought with it a realisation of the terrible damage. 'Himmelpforten had simply ceased to exist ... Some of the trees on the road into Günne had railway lines wrapped round them like corkscrews. The flotsam had stripped away all the bark; they were standing there like white ghosts.'

The breach at the Möhne had already caused havoc. Neheim, a few miles from the dam, was overwhelmed in the early hours at about 0110. It was the first significant population point below the Möhne dam. Industrial buildings stood on its banks close by the water, while from slightly higher up – very fortunately as it turned out – the impressive facade of the church of Saint John the Baptist stood guard on the streets and the square below.

Then the floods hit Neheim, its coalfields and ironworks were swamped. Most of the inhabitants affected spent the night out in the open, camping out in the hills. Fifty-one men, sixty-six women and thirty children lost their lives in the town. In addition, 444 livestock were killed. Dortmund, further off and therefore better placed to receive warnings, later experienced major problems. The city's air-raid shelters were flooded and nearly half the citizens were forced out into the night. For a time the only way to get around many of the streets of the city was in a flat-bottomed boat.

One of the problems in Neheim was that, despite several telephoned warnings, the authorities there refused to accept that the dam had been breached. There were no organised flood-warning measures in place and this undoubtedly added to the loss of life. One resident, Hermann Kaiser, went down into the air-raid shelter in the cellar when warnings of enemy activity in the area were received about midnight.

Kaiser was there with his three sisters, the housemaid and a Russian cook, Anna: his parents were away visiting as Sunday had been Mother's Day. Anna, the cook, was a widow who had been brought in as a conscripted worker by the Germans. After the noise from the planes flying over the town had died down, she went back to her room.

The others were down in the cellar when they heard the phone ring. The housemaid went to answer it but hurried back down to tell them that she could hear a terrible splashing and rattling noise. Then their nerves were shattered as their gardener, Josef Greis, burst in, shouting, 'Get out! Get out! Everyone out of here now!'

Greis then rushed to Anna's room and hammered on the door but she would not answer it. The others ran out of the house in a panic. They managed to make their way up a hill where hundreds of others had also gathered. It all happened in a matter of minutes and there were very narrow margins determining whether an individual survived or not. Kaiser looked on with disbelief as he saw a river 'as wide as the Mississippi' rolling down the valley making a noise 'like 25 express trains'. The cook, Anna, was found drowned in the laundry room the next morning having been washed there from her room. There were no signs that she had tried to save herself. Perhaps the misery of a conscripted labourer's life meant that there was nothing much left for her to fight for.

Ferdi Dröge was a sixteen-year-old apprentice living in Neheim. Like many others, when he heard the air-raid warnings he had made his way to the shelter, where he reckoned there were about 200 others present. They had sat on planks and beer barrels, playing cards and eating snacks, waiting out the boredom of the raids. Then an acquaintance, Johannes Kessler, ran in and told them to get out at once, shouting that 'the Möhne's had it'. They made their way out as quickly as possible and had enough time to reach higher ground and safety.

The civilian loss in Neheim was bad enough but would be surpassed by a scene of even greater horror. In the town there was a labour camp just above the river with a number of Ukrainian female inmates. As the war progressed, the Germans had found it increasingly difficult to obtain enough labour to run the war economy. Eventually they had turned to the expedient of forcibly recruiting labour from the territories they had occupied in the east.

About 1,200 women from Ukraine and Poland had arrived at Soest railway station in the early summer of 1943 and had then been transferred to Neheim. The camp on the edge of Neheim was established to support an armaments factory. It was at the foot of the Wiedenburg, a hill above the Möhne. That night, the alarm had gone off about midnight and shortly thereafter low-flying aircraft had passed over and shot up the barracks. Even before this night, some had wondered whether the camp was too close to the river and might be susceptible to floods. They were about to have their suspicions confirmed with terrifying effect.

Just over an hour after the alarm had been heard, a fearsome roaring was heard approaching the camp. Then, as eyes began to focus in the bright moonlight, a wall of water could be seen descending on the camp. Some of the inmates were ordered out of their buildings and told to run towards safety. They began to panic and had to be threatened with pistols to keep them in check. Some though did manage to escape the floods by moving out of their way. But many it seems never made it out of their barrack blocks.

One of the workers was a Ukrainian woman, Darja Michajlowna Moros. When she heard the air-raid alarms she took no notice; in this period of intensive RAF activity, they were a regular occurrence and she was getting fed up with them and the disturbance to her sleep that they resulted in. However, when it was realised that the dam had broken, the inmates were let out and ran for their lives.

The camp was surrounded by barbed wire, which meant that there was a bottleneck by the gate where all the women were trying to get out. There was an old guard there, a man with a limp. The inmates knew him as Robert. He got out a pair of pliers and cut the barbed wire so that more of the women could get out and try to outrun the waters. Sadly he himself could not and this unsung hero was lost in the floods.

Amid the tragedy, there was one remarkable story that shed a small ray of light on the gloom. Karl Josef Stüppardt was a guard at the camp and while he was there he fell in love with one of the women, named Elena, who came from Sibéria though she had lived most of her life in Ukraine. His feelings were reciprocated and the unlikely couple used to meet regularly, occasionally even having illicit nights out at the nearby cinema, where Elena learned German.

On the night of the flood, Stüppardt ran into the camp trying to rouse the women. Many of them did not take him seriously but eventually some did try and make their escape. Elena was one of them and she managed to get away dressed only in a slip with an overcoat on top. She survived though Stüppardt found himself in a different kind of deep water when it was discovered that he had been fraternising with one of the foreign workers, something that was strictly against Germany's race laws.

Nevertheless, he managed to stay in touch with Elena and this story did have a truly happy ending. On 16 June 1945, barely a month after the war ended, Stüppardt and Elena were married in the church of Saint John the Baptist. The church was overflowing, with many of the congregation being recently released Russian prisoners. Many surely remembered that in the very same building, just over two years before, the pews had been moved to one side so that the interior could be used for the terrible business of laying out the dead whose bodies had been recovered after the deluge.

Any thoughts of romance or joy lay far in the distant and uncertain future on this most awful of nights. Now, Ferdi Dröge looked on in horror as he heard the screams of the women workers trying to get away from the floods. He could see a huge wave surging down:

> [It] looked like a black block of flats with terraces; it was full of trees, pieces of wood and animals. That pitch-black wall of water coming towards me was at least 12 metres high; in it, and looking as if they were stacked on top of each other, were sections of wooden huts and people screaming. Dotted around in amongst those whirling bits of weed were little lights which went out in the spray. I was no more than 200 metres from the leading edge of that wave.

A few hundred women at least were saved but hundreds of others died. Residents later insisted that the barracks had been swept away with their residents still trapped inside, but they were smashed to pieces on a concrete bridge downstream; the screams of the doomed could still be heard as their flimsy protection was torn apart and they met their deaths.

Dröge, an articulate witness who gave a vivid account of what he had seen, spoke of how the floods overwhelmed a transformer station and a colossal flash lit up the valley. As he managed to escape further uphill, he followed the tragedy down in the valley: 'the crashing, the roaring, the smashing and the death cries. Seen from the side, the first giant wave looked like steps. Each wall of water rose up above the one in front as the torrent thrust its way down the valley.' The marks made by the floodwater suggested that in places it was 45 feet deep. A huge mass of rock, some 18 metres long by 5 metres high, was gouged out by the floods.

One of the residents of Neheim, Josef Rösen, had seen the sky in the north-east glowing brightly just before the deluge descended and at once thought of the dam. He ran into the house and woke his sister, having the presence of mind to ask her to collect some drinking water and candles. Then he heard a roar in the distance; over it he could hear people screaming and animals bleating. He went down to the town which was already a scene of chaos. Bodies were already swirling around in the waters that were deluging the town.

Rösen heard voices coming from the mist that had formed as a result of the huge volume of water. Looking up in the branches of a tree, he saw several completely naked women – survivors from the Ukrainian women at the nearby camp. He got them down from the tree and then to safety. He then made a basic raft out of doors and timbers and ferried those he could to safety.

He too was a hero, though he would in the aftermath witness the evidence of the horrific end that some of those in the area had suffered. There was, for example, the devoted mother who had gone down to rescue her six-year-old son from the waters after she had safely got her other children to the attic; neither of them could escape the rising waters and they both drowned in their living room. In another case, fifty people had been trapped in an air-raid shelter and had been unable to open the door because of the rising waters outside. They all drowned.

The German authorities were already putting a picture together, though at the moment it was fragmented and unclear. By 0108, Hilse, the chief of police at Soest (although only a few miles away, the town was safely protected from the floods by a screen of hills), reached the Möhne dam and saw that the wall was already seriously damaged. Just a few minutes after the breach, Oberföster Wilkening had run to the Ruhr-Lippe Railway, the site of the nearest telephone that he was aware of, to phone through a flood warning; there was a phone system at the Möhne direct to Soest but it had been destroyed in the attack; it had maybe been destroyed by Hopgood's blast.

As the drama continued to unfold, the main focus of the activity shifted. In contrast to the sense of triumph felt by those who had successfully breached the dam, now came the tragedy. The main actions were now being played out in the valley below the Möhne dam as cataclysmic events unfolded, bringing death and destruction in their wake.

In the skies not far above, the planes either made their way back towards safety, though their peril was as yet far from over, or pushed on towards the next objective if they had not yet dropped their bombs. Back at Grantham, after the elation following the receipt of Gibson's confirmatory message that the wall at the Möhne dam had been broken, a waiting game began once more. Following that message, there would be no further communication with the raiders for 48 minutes. But the mood was lightened as the senior figures at Grantham knew for sure that one of the three major operational objectives had been achieved.

But the evening's toll was far from over. At about 0115, the residents of Hemfurth, some miles to the south-east of the Möhne reservoir, were woken by the noise of low-flying aircraft. Gibson and the other planes that remained behind had flown on from the Möhne dam to the Eder reservoir, which was about 43 miles away. Unlike that at the Möhne, the Eder dam was unguarded – flak guns, until recently sited on the wall, had been removed just a week before. However, it had extremely strong natural defences. The position of the dam would make it very difficult indeed for the attackers to get into the right position to release their bombs as it was surrounded by very steep hills.

It was at about 0130 that the attack on the Eder dam really began. There were five planes remaining, though only three of them were carrying bombs. Both Gibson and Young were bomb-less. Gibson's job was to act once more as the master bomber and Young's to take over should anything happen to him. Those with bombs were the planes flown by Shannon, Knight and Maudslay (AJ-L, AJ-N and AJ-Z respectively).

The dam had not been easy to find as fog was now starting to build up. It took Gibson five circles around the area to locate the structure. The Eder dam was surrounded by dark hills guarded by platoons of pine trees, sentinels ready to do their part in repelling all uninvited intruders. But the fact that there were no anti-aircraft guns there was reassuring as reconnaissance photos had suggested there might be – but the objects seen from the air were in fact trees.

Gibson radioed Shannon to make his run first, using the message 'Cooler 6'. This was, however, easier said than done as Shannon was not sure where he was. This was not surprising as the dam was hidden away among hills and forests and was not easy to find. Gibson therefore told Hutchison, his wireless operator, to set off a red flare, which he did. Shannon could see it at once and moved into position.

Shannon had found a target not long before but it was in fact the wrong one. After making the short flight from the Möhne dam, Shannon's bomb had been left spinning. Those who were to attack the dam were faced with a formidable proposition. There were several challenges facing those attacking at the Eder, including the fact that there was no model of the dam available until after the raid. There were only reconnaissance photos to go from and estimates of height from these were out by up to 125 feet.

The fog was growing thick over the Eder dam too and it was hard to tell a valley filled with water from one filled with fog, especially in the enclosed landscape surrounding the reservoir. Gibson had become separated from the other planes on the way in and now called them up. Gibson's Very light over the dam alerted not only Shannon but the others in the flight too.

At the far end of the dam, and high above the water, was a magnificent Gothic castle. As the dam was surrounded by hills, the planes would have to fly in over this castle at 1,000 feet and would then have to drop rapidly to 60 feet for the final approach for the attack. Much greater flying skills were needed for this raid than the one on the Möhne dam, even though there were no defences in situ. Once passing hard a-port over a spit of land in the lake, there were just seven seconds left to get into the right position for an attack on the dam and the Lancaster was a big, heavy plane that it was difficult to get into exactly the right spot.

Shannon moved in for his approach. At least there were no enemy gunners to distract him here, which was just as well given the extent of the challenges facing him. He flew over the castle on the hill at Waldeck and then dropped sharply to 60 feet. He then had to turn sharply to port to complete the final, short approach to the dam wall. However, his bomb-aimer, Sergeant Les Sumpter, was not happy with the approach so they circled again. As Shannon ascended again rapidly, forced to pull up to fly over the hills at the far end of the dam that were covered in a blanket of trees, he had to do so at full boost; Gibson could see sparks coming from his engine as the plane strained upwards. Shannon came back for four more attempts and was unable to make a suitable approach on each occasion.

Unsurprisingly, these repeated aborted attempts to get into just the right spot were very unsettling for Shannon, who later recalled that 'to get out of the valley after crossing the dam wall we had to put on full throttle and do a steep climbing turn to avoid a vast rock face'. As Gibson looked on, he decided that it might be better to give someone else a go and see if they had better luck.

So as Shannon was about to line up another run, Gibson told Maudslay to take his place and make an attempt. It did not, however, make any difference, for Maudslay also took two approaches and was unsuccessful. Shannon was then directed to try again. He was finding the approach very difficult and he still could not get his aircraft in the right place to drop his bomb.

The problem was that the route to be followed called for real precision flying and there was very little margin of error. The descent from Waldeck castle was not directly towards the lake but over a spur of land called the Hammerberg. Once beyond the dam there was a sizeable hill, the Michelskopf, over which the planes would have to climb sharply. This would be no mean feat, especially if the planes had to abort an approach with a bomb still on board; it would in the end take eleven attempts to drop three bombs at the Eder.

Some way behind the planes over the Eder, the third wave was starting to arrive over the Continent. At 0130 Ken Brown flew over the Dutch coast in AJ-F. He was, however, a long way off course – his compass may have been wrong. He was followed over the coast by Bill Townsend, just a minute behind. They pushed on towards their objectives, though at this stage they were still not sure exactly where they would be. It depended to some extent on how well Gibson and the remaining crews got on at the Eder.

In the meantime, closer to Gibson's next target it was now becoming clearer that something was amiss. At 0132 the telephone rang in the local air-raid defence office near the Eder dam. It was answered by Leutnant Saahr of the SS. He was told that there were British aircraft circling over the dam. He rang the Third Company of the 603rd Regional Defence Battalion (SS) at Hemfurth, the village below the dam, to get confirmation of the fact, which was duly given. Saahr then rang Colonel Karl Bürke of the SS Flak Training Regiment to tell him that a flood may well be imminent. Bürke put 100 men on standby with lorries. Saahr phoned back almost at once to say that the planes were dropping flares so they had had searchlights switched on.

At 0139 Shannon moved back in for his attack on the Eder. Sumpter was this time happy with the approach and the bomb was dropped, bouncing twice and sinking as it hit the dam wall. The fact that it bounced twice may suggest that the bomb was released too early. About a minute after the bomb was released, there was an explosion and a spout of water about 1,000 feet high. A gap about 9 feet wide was seen on the east side of the dam by Shannon. Wireless officer Brian Goodale signalled back 'Goner 79B', which meant a small breach in the Eder dam.

However, Gibson was not convinced and later reported back that he could see no apparent damage from this strike. Shannon was just glad to get out of there; he later described the attack as 'a bugger of a job'. The exit over the Michelskopf, with the bomb still attached on three occasions, was described as 'bloody hairy'. He had at least survived the attack, but so too had the Eder dam. Now Gibson had just two bombs left to drop (ignoring any that might be available from the reserve wave) to complete the task at the Eder and return home in veritable triumph.

Despite the success at the Möhne dam, Gibson cannot have been confident at this stage of repeating the trick here. Extreme flying was called for if the bomb were to be dropped in the right spot and, if it were not, then he could not be sure of success. Each dam had its own specific challenge; at the Möhne it was the flak guns, at the Eder the difficulty of the approach. The mission was proving every bit as difficult a challenge as expected and costs had already been high (though Gibson at this stage only knew of Hopgood's loss for certain). The sacrifices had not ended yet, either for those in the air or those on the land beneath them.

7

Breach of Eder Dam: Dinghy at Target Y

01.46–02.00, Monday 17 May

Even as the attack on the Eder dam was intensifying, the effects of the Möhne breach in the meantime were continuing to worsen. From Wickede, a few miles further downstream from Neheim, the planes flying over for earlier attacks on the dams could be clearly seen in the bright moonlight. There were though no reports of any serious breaches for a while and when Clemens Mols, the postmaster, went to find out if anything of significance had happened, all he heard was that planes were now flying low over the Eder. He therefore assumed that the danger had passed. Mols returned to his family, among whom the mood was now calm.

However, urged on by his wife, Mols went back to the post office to see if he could find out more and while he was there the phone rang. When he answered it, he found that it was the postmaster from nearby Arnsberg (also close to Neheim but safe from the flood as it was not on the river) on the line. He asked Mols incredulously why he was still there when the water was now in Vosswinkel, just 5 kilometres away from Wickede. Mols at once hurried back home and told his wife to get up to the high ground while he tried to wake people up by phone.

He tried to do this but with no success. In the meantime, his wife returned and begged him to come up to the high ground with her. He agreed but they had barely started on the journey when a fog appeared. Mols recognised this as a forerunner of the water and realised that they could not outrun it so they rushed back into the house and hurried upstairs. They were barely in time as the foaming waters followed them into the house.

They managed to carry bedding and clothes up into the attic, hoping that the walls would not give way against the weight of the water and also that the waters would not rise high enough to submerge it. Above them, the moon shone down brightly while the terrifying sound of low-flying aircraft could be heard, though no further bombs were dropped. Frau Mols was beside herself and all her husband could do was try and reassure her to keep her calm.

Off to the south-east and some miles away, at 0146 Henry Maudslay ('Cooler 7') began his attack on the Eder dam. His aircraft had possibly been damaged on the way in as something had been seen hanging under the bomb-bay. The approach was difficult and the precision required to drop the bomb in the exact place pinpoint. The reservoir was in fact a long, serpentine lake with inlets and tree-girt promontories sticking out like long fingers of land into the water. It was impossible to get a straight run into the dam and very easy to be past it before you knew it. This was certainly a far harder attack technically than that on the Möhne dam.

Maudslay manoeuvred his plane into position as well as he could and swooped down towards the dam. It was a great boon that there was no flak, but the sheerness of the hills round about more than compensated for the lack of opposition. Here nature was the greatest enemy and the sculpting of the hills would prove the most significant obstacle that had to be overcome.

Gibson watched closely, silently urging Maudslay and his crew on, willing them to succeed, inwardly telling them to maintain the right height, hold their course, keep their nerve. Even as he did so, Maudslay's plane briefly climbed, as if trying to avoid something, perhaps a treetop, before dropping back down again.

Maudslay would have very little time to get his plane into the right position and split-second timing was called for. In the event, his bomb appeared to leave the aircraft late. The bomb bounced too high and bounced over the parapet rather than hitting the dam. It detonated seconds afterwards as the plane was still over it. 'There was a slow, yellow, vivid flame which lit up the whole valley like daylight for just a few seconds,' Gibson remarked later.

Maudslay's plane was illuminated by the explosion, the shock from which may well have hit his plane. Given the late release of the bomb, Gibson's comments concerning Maudslay's sudden unexpected, albeit temporary, climb on the approach may assume extra significance. Perhaps it broke Maudslay's concentration and this led to the mistimed drop. Maybe it is even possible that he had clipped something that had caused some damage. As neither plane nor crew members would make it back to England to tell the tale, no one will ever know.

That exactly happened to Maudslay's plane is veiled in mystery though it did not crash at the dam. However, it may well have been damaged and this could have affected the performance of the aircraft, either on the way into the final approach or as a result of the blast – very possibly from both events. It was always regarded as a risk that a plane might be affected by the blast should it be in the wrong place at the wrong time: two planes had after all been damaged late on in the training stage because they had been hit by the columns of water thrown up during practice. It would be no surprise if the impact of a bomb blast had seriously damaged Maudslay's plane.

The plane limped on in the direction of Emmerich, close to the Dutch border near Nijmegen. Gibson tried to make contact over the radio but the signal from Maudslay's plane was very weak; when asked if he was alright, the reply faintly came, 'I think so.' Gibson had in fact lost sight of Maudslay: he was also worried as even now the sky was starting to subtly brighten as dawn drew closer and they were running out of time to complete the raid and certainly to return to England without a gravely increased risk of being intercepted. Maudslay flew off, now on his own, while Gibson returned to the immediate task of coordinating the raid on the Eder dam. However, Maudslay's 'Goner 28B' message (attack at Eder dam, bomb overshot, no apparent breach) was received at Grantham at 0157, confirming that he and his crew were still very much alive at this time.

Even with their VHF radios, communication between the crews was still fragmentary. At 0151 Gibson tried to raise Astell but there was no response as he had been dead for nearly two hours. As well as being worried about his fellow pilot, Gibson would also have been very aware that there was only one bomb left and it had to work if the Eder dam was to be successfully breached (though there was always the option of deploying planes from the reserve wave should the dam remain unbreached).

At 0152 Les Knight prepared for his attack on the Eder. As he had the last bomb remaining from the first wave, this was a particularly high-pressure moment. Like the other pilots who had attacked the Eder, Knight had great trouble negotiating the right angle for his approach. He tried the approach once but the run was aborted as the plane was not in a satisfactory position (it was in fact going too fast at 240 mph).

There was a flow back and forth of chatter over the radio with advice, more or less helpful, being given by those who had already made the run or watched one being made. Shannon was especially voluble – Les Sumpter recalled that 'Dave was talking to him, telling him how to do it, and Les Knight told him to get off the air'. Knight wanted no distractions as he concentrated fully on ensuring that he and his crew were working together seamlessly to get the plane where it needed to be to drop the bomb in perfect position.

Knight and his crew were effectively on their own, with the last bomb on board and the Eder dam before them still standing firm and defiant. He did though have perfect visibility with the moon to starboard. But the dam was proving very hard to attack and even Gibson was beginning to think that the approach was too difficult.

Gibson was on the point of giving up when Knight made one final run. Once more he hopped over a high hill on the way in towards the dam, an interruption to a clear run in that greatly added to the complexity of the approach. Knight took an approach route slightly to the east of that planned, where the hill known as the Hammerberg was lower and the distance to the dam beyond it greater. This gave him vital extra seconds to ensure that he was in the right place to drop the bomb.

This time the approach was perfect and the calculation of the dropping spot for the bomb precise. Gibson, alongside, saw the bomb bounce three times and then explode. Flight Sergeant Robert Kellow, the wireless operator in Knight's plane, AJ-N, looked back at the dam. 'It was still intact for a short while, then as if some huge fist had been jabbed at the wall, a large, almost round black hole appeared and water gushed as if from a long hose.'

To Gibson it was 'as if a gigantic hand had punched a hole through cardboard'. In fact, Knight's last run was the best Gibson had witnessed of the whole night. It had indeed been a masterclass of split-second timing and perfect positioning. Knight had dropped his bomb and there was what seemed like a tremendous earthquake soon after. Then the whole dam collapsed like a pack of cards. Knight was in no mood to celebrate just yet; at the end of the run, Knight 'had to climb like buggery to get out' because of the steep hills behind the dam. Celebration could come later; at this particular moment survival came first as Knight and Ray Grayston, his flight engineer, pulled hard on the controls to get the plane climbing as quickly as possible.

On this occasion, there was no confusion or delay in the relaying of information back to Grantham. Pilot Officer Bob Kellow radioed back 71B, 'large breach in dam'. Those on board could see a spout of water 800 feet high shooting up above the dam. Then a tide of water 30 feet high was seen travelling down the valley, smashing buildings and bridges in its path. The workers on the steps of the generator plant below the dam felt the building shake. They ran down to the main room but the lighting had failed. Masonry fell from the ceiling and water started to rush in but they managed to reach the stone steps up before the dam burst completely open.

Werner Salz was a fitter at the power stations named Hemfurth I and II right by the dam, down at its very foot. He had been out on the Saturday night but was not long in bed when he heard planes flying over. Getting up, he could see that four-engined aircraft were flying so low that he claimed that the crews could be seen in the cockpit.

He witnessed several explosions before, following a third, he felt the ground shake. He realised that the dam had been hit, a belief that was confirmed when he heard the sound of rushing water. Thinking that the power stations had been hit, he ran back to Hemfurth. When he arrived there he could see that water was already lapping around the houses.

'I ran to the dam to see how big the breach was. It was huge. Masses of water were thundering out – a catastrophe.' He was worried about his workmates. He wondered if they had drowned. He could see two men flashing lights from the roof of the control room at Hemfurth I. Of his four workmates, three would survive but Jakob Kurtze, a machinist, could not be found. His body was found in August that year under a mass of gravel. The survival of the other three, who were right underneath the huge breach, was quite extraordinary.

Below the dam, Karl Albrecht was the engineer of one of the two power stations. Water and debris began to pour through the roof of the building he was in. He rushed up the steps to the parapet of the dam, just in time to see the breach widen and the water pour through into the valley below (the key to his survival perhaps therefore appears to be that the breach progressively got larger, giving him time to make good his escape, rather than the wall collapsing at once). The phone lines were cut by the deluge soon after, though some early warning was possible before this happened. The postmaster at Bad Wildungen, to the south of the Eder reservoir and out of harm's way, was able to phone warnings further down the valley and saved a number of lives in the process. By now, a wave 30 feet high was raging down the valley.

Again the topography of the area was important in the sequence of events that followed. The water which poured through the shattered dam wall had a steep drop into the valley below. Once it hit the valley floor it would be hemmed in for some way by very steep, almost precipitous, rocky hills on one side and less steep but still significant contours on the other. This meant that, trapped as it was, the water would build up tremendous force as it surged down the valley. Fortunately, the Eder valley was less populated than the Möhne and this would result in a far smaller loss of life here.

At 0154 the 'Dinghy' signal was sent, the code word to tell those back at Grantham that the Eder too had been broken. Interestingly, Kellow's 'Goner 710B' message confirming that AJ-N's plane had dropped its bomb and caused a large breach at the Eder dam was not sent until 0200, six minutes after Gibson's 'Dinghy' message had been sent. This hints at one of the less successful elements of the raids, that of long-distance communications, though this element of it is often overlooked. Nevertheless, the problem may have had some significance, especially in the coordination and targeting of the third wave. It certainly also suggests that discipline concerning this element of the raids was more lax, and perhaps the training less effective, than other elements of the mission: Joe McCarthy's wireless operator, Flight Sergeant Leonard Eaton, would not report the dropping of the bomb at the Sorpe dam until several hours after it had happened.

There was nothing further for Gibson to do now but to try everything he could to get everyone back to base safely. His offensive mission was over and it was up to the reserve planes to do as best they could with, in the event, little coordination between them. Gibson ordered all the remaining planes in his flight home and promised them he would meet them in the mess afterwards 'for the biggest party of all time'. 'Good show boys, let's all go home and get pie,' were the words he remembered.

As the crews who had breached the Eder dam headed home, they followed the now-released waters down the steep valley in what looked like a 30-foot wall of water. It obliterated power stations and submerged roads as it went. They saw lights being extinguished, 'like a great black shadow had been drawn across the earth', a vision of hell that a number of the crews looking on witnessed. Down below, the pilots could see car headlights being submerged and extinguished beneath the unstoppable torrent that was now cascading down the valley. According to Leonard Sumpter 'down there somewhere we could see cars going along and the water went over the car headlights and just drowned them.'

However, for all the euphoria there was still great danger for those pilots who had not yet managed to return to British airspace. At 0157 Henry Maudslay's wireless operator Aiden Cottam sent a message back to 5 Group. It was very weak but gave the code 'Goner 28B', which means 'special weapon released, overshot dam, no apparent breach'. It was the last communication received from the plane.

There were now two dams successfully breached, but there were in all three main targets and three secondary ones identified by the British as potential objectives. The night's action was not yet over. There was still a third, reserve wave heading for the Ruhr. At around 0145 a flak warning was transmitted to this third group. The German defences would have been well on their guard now, something that was about to be proved with dramatic effect.

Going the other way, at 0153 David Maltby flew out to safety over the North Sea. At almost exactly the same time as Maltby and his men could start to relax to a certain extent, Lewis Burpee and his crew in AJ-S were shot down while heading towards Germany, an act witnessed by Ken Brown in AJ-F. This happened near Tilburg between Breda and Eindhoven in the Netherlands.

Burpee was about a mile off course, making his way towards the Sorpe dam (again emphasising the difficulty of exact navigation and the potentially fatal consequences of a small margin of error). When only 25 metres above the ground, Burpee's plane was caught in a searchlight at the Gilze-Rijen Luftwaffe base in the Netherlands, a heavily defended spot. Gilze-Rijen was a Dutch army airfield taken over by the Germans earlier in the war when they had overrun the Netherlands. There were nine Messerschmitt Bf 110G night fighters based there and seven Junkers JU-88Cs.

Dazzled by the searchlights that caught him as he approached the base, Burpee tried to avoid the flak at the airfield by flying still lower but his plane clipped the trees. He lost control and crashed into the airbase, ploughing into a Military Transport post where fire and other trucks were stored. There was a huge explosion; all the crew in the plane were killed instantly. Windows and doors around the base were blown in. Ammunition explosions added to the cacophony. Burpee had at least succeeded in disabling the radar base on the station but had paid the ultimate price for it.

Lewis Burpee was a Canadian, born in 1918. He had flown his first mission in October 1942 in a raid on Cologne and went on his first raid in charge of his own plane a month later in an aborted foray to Genoa. Being in the last reserve wave he had, like others in that group, followed the same southerly route taken by Gibson's wave on the way out to the region of the dams. He had been looking for a known gap in the air defences between two night-fighter bases at Eindhoven and Gilze-Rijen. As the defences would have been on alert after the earlier waves had flown their missions, members of the third wave were in especial danger. Burpee's wife was pregnant with their first child, who would be born that Christmas. He would also be named Lewis after the father he would never see.

Ken Brown, a fellow Canadian, witnessed Burpee's demise. There was at least one more positive outcome from what had happened. Seeing Burpee hit alerted Brown to danger and he was able to steer clear of trouble. When he flew over, the whole valley where Burpee had crashed was lit up by an orange flame. Brown dived to avoid danger and followed the course of a road when all of a sudden two turrets loomed ahead, either side of a castle. Brown managed to fly between them and on towards his target.

Stefan Oancia was the bomb-aimer in Brown's plane, which was about 10 miles behind Burpee's, and saw that 'Burpee's Lancaster ahead of us flew over a German airfield and was hit by ground fire, fuel tanks exploding and a ball of flame rising slowly – stopping, then dropping terminated by a huge ball of flame as it hit the ground and the bomb exploded' – a succinct but informative description of what had happened.

Oancia could see quite clearly what was happening. He could see the tracer rising up from the airfield, he saw it stop when it hit the aircraft and then he saw the plane in flames. He believed that Burpee had been hit, as he witnessed the plane start to climb before it then plummeted to the ground as if the plane were completely out of control. But not all witnesses saw events this way.

Herbert Scholl was a wireless operator at the base. He said that the night-fighter crews were on standby in front of their barracks when a plane flew over (the second one that had flown over the base that night). Suddenly it was lit up by a searchlight. The plane, already low, dropped even lower into the trees, where it crashed to the ground, slamming into an empty military vehicle garage.

There was then a tremendous explosion. The shockwaves knocked the night-fighter crews 600–700 feet away off their feet. Scholl was adamant that no flak had been fired (in contrast to Oancia's account) and that this was a rare account of 'kill by a searchlight'. But another eyewitness mentioned the flak too, though also accepting that it was the searchlight's blinding light that caused the plane to crash.

The next morning, those on the base inspected the wreckage. The body of the rear gunner in the plane, Warrant Officer Joseph Bradley (another Canadian), showed hardly any sign of injury. Those there noticed that he was dressed in lace-up shoes with worn out soles and thin, unpressed uniform trousers.

Brown though had managed to get through without damage. Later, as they moved on, Brown instructed his gunners to open up on a train moving up a gentle slope in order to ensure that everything was in working order with the guns. But not everyone was happy with the way things were going; Basil Feneron, the flight engineer in AJ-F, felt that they were not flying low enough and were therefore at risk of being shot down.

Brown and his crew had though survived and carried on to their designated target. This was to be the Sorpe dam, still standing defiantly after having so far suffered only one hit. Brown was at least now approaching it and could do his best to succeed where McCarthy had failed. The scene was set for the final acts of this extraordinarily dramatic night. To be a complete success, the Sorpe needed to be breached, adding significantly to the chaos already unleashed on the Ruhr and its vital infrastructure.

8

Chaos in the Möhne & Eder Valleys

02.01–03.00, Monday 17 May

The scene of the drama now switched once more from the pilots who had released their bombs to the victims of the terror that had been put in train when the dams were burst asunder. Now, there were two dams breached and millions of gallons of water had been released with no possibility of stopping the deluge until it had worn itself out. A number of towns were under water within an hour of the breach – some within minutes. For many the horror would last through the entire night and beyond.

Freed from the walls that had held them in check, the waters surged down the valleys beneath the dams, searching out the line of least resistance and overwhelming anything or anyone in their path. After the raids, there would be much debate about how effective the mission had been. These discussions tended to look at such matters at the strategic level, ignoring their personal impact on those in the way of the waters. There is no debate whatsoever about the scale of the horror that overwhelmed all those unfortunate enough to be in the path of the inundation.

The water of course was indiscriminate as to its victims, young or old, male or female. In Hemfurth, a mile or so down a steep and winding road from the Eder dam, fourteen-year-old Wilfried Albrecht had been woken by his mother and rushed out into the street. He saw not only boats but also boathouses coming through the gap in the dam wall. One of the first to die was his workmate at the power station who had sought shelter in the cellars there, not reckoning that the dam wall would break. His body was found months later 20 kilometres downstream.

Nearby, Elise Schäfer was also woken by her mother. The day before had been Mothering Sunday, a lovely, sunny day which, according to her father, promised a bumper harvest in the autumn. Her father peered out of the window and saw something, suggestive of a cloud, in the distance. He was not sure what it was but he knew it was not a normal cloud and he was worried. They went out into the street and in the distance they heard the distinct sound of rushing water. Two schoolboys appeared, spreading the alarming tidings that the water was coming. Unsure whether to believe them or not, they had their worst fears confirmed when a soldier approached them, telling them that it was all too true.

Elise went up the stairs to fetch her grandfather, who was on the upper floor. By the time she got down again, everyone else was gone and she was on her own. She rushed back in and went back upstairs to join her grandfather. Fortunately, the water did not rise high enough to submerge the house, which also stood firm against the buffeting it received from large chunks of wreckage that were hurled against it by the water.

Emma Becker was sheltered in an air-raid shelter nearby. She had been to a civil defence meeting on the previous evening where ironically the subject of a raid on the dam had been broached. A warden had assured them that the dam would never be hit and on no account should anyone leave a shelter during a raid. It was poor advice and it could have cost Emma her life. It was also another example of the complacency and tunnel vision that characterised the German authorities' approach to the possibility of a raid.

Suddenly, Emma's neighbour, Herr Kohl, rushed in saying that everyone should evacuate the cellar at once as the dam had been hit and rushing water could be heard moving in their direction. She ran out of the shelter with her son, only to find that she had been parted from her daughter. Running back into the house she found the child was still there, so terrified that it was as if she were frozen to the spot. She dragged her out of the house behind her like a sack.

Then I saw the first wave coming across the nearby playing field. It was about six metres high and as white as snow. We ran up a hill behind our house, but there was a fence in the way. We lifted the children over and were pulling and tearing at the fence when the floodwater caught up with us. What a miracle! The fence gave way and we were safe.

For the civilian population in Germany, the deluge was starting to hit home. It was around 0200, soon after the Eder was breached, when the phone rang in Colonel Bürke's office (Bürke was the officer of an SS flak unit in the area). It was Leutnant Saahr of the local air-raid warning office saying that he had received a message that the dam had been destroyed. The village nearest the dam had already been alerted. A motorcyclist tore up the main street of Affoldern, a couple of miles down the valley from Hemfurth right on the banks of the Eder river, telling people 'the dam has been hit, the water is coming, everyone out of the cellars quickly'. The villagers got out of the cellars as quickly as they could and headed for the nearest high ground. The water sped through and soon after demolished the suspension bridge at Hemelfort.

The villagers of Nieder-Werbe, who lived right by the reservoir, had naturally been alarmed while the raids were on. They were at least very fortunate in living above the dam rather than below it. Now they were startled to see the lake level dropping in front of their very eyes. One of the villagers, Fritz Fesseler, a soldier home on leave, jumped on his motorbike and roared along the road that ran alongside the lake. He had the presence of mind to take his camera with him, but he was so overwhelmed by the scene unfolding before him that after taking one magnificent photograph he forgot to wind it on and ruined the rest of the film.

The residents of Mehlen lived about 8 kilometres downstream from the Eder dam, just past Affoldern. One of them was August Kötter, a soldier who had only returned from the Russian front the night before and must have been looking forward to some peace and quiet and blissful domesticity compared to the horrors he had been used to. He had gone to bed at midnight after an evening with family and friends when he was woken by shouts that the dam had been hit.

At first he was disbelieving; he did not think breaching the dam would be easy and before he had left for Russia there had been anti-aircraft guns in place defending it and he was unaware that they had been moved. Having got up to see what was happening once the planes flew off, he went back to bed. He was not there long before screaming outside told him that the dam had been breached. While those already up started to run for cover up the nearby hills, Kötter went to fetch his pig from the sty and brought it into the house with him.

His children had run off up the hill but he now realised that it was too late for him and his wife (and the pig) to escape. He could see a wave coming on, 'like an avalanche', about 3 metres high. A great wave smashed his front door open and he struggled, up to his chest in water, to the staircase to the upper storey of his house. He could hear the pig squealing in the water and it was washed out of the house through an open window.

He and his wife made it to the attic. He managed to remove some roof tiles so that he could look outside and see what was happening. The experience became progressively more terrifying; the pressure of the water washed the side of the house away and then the front of the building caved in. Fearing that the rest would follow, Kötter tried to cobble up a raft with which to float across to a nearby house which was relatively undamaged. However, it did not function effectively and they had to stay put and take their chances where they were. Remarkably, the house did not completely collapse; photographs taken after the waters subsided show the remains of a building seemingly perched half in mid-air as if held up by nothing save matchsticks.

Fortunately, this particular vignette had several happy endings. Kötter and his wife were both rescued and even the pig survived, rescued by a nearby farmer and put in his sty for safekeeping. The pig and Kötter's wife were reunited soon after, the animal running joyfully back to her when it recognised her voice. Whether or not this affected the pig's long-term survival prospects is sadly not recorded, but given food shortages in the area in the aftermath of the devastation it seems highly unlikely.

In the meantime, the crews who had caused the damage were now focused on making their way back to England. The reserve wave, however, ploughed resolutely on. Their targets were flexible but, though in some ways such flexibility was not only desirable but essential, the lack of a clear briefing on the reserve targets would prove problematic. This would prove one of the weaker parts of the plan developed by Bomber Command.

With both the Möhne and the Eder dams gone now, clearly the next priority was the Sorpe. (In fact, economically it was a much higher priority than the Eder and the fact that it was not attacked more systematically by either the remaining planes from the first wave once the Möhne had been breached, or en masse by the reserve wave, was odd.)

Hindsight would suggest that this dam could in fact not be breached using the technology available on the raid but this was not recognised in the official orders, although conversations in advance of the raid suggested that it was always recognised as a tougher nut to crack due to its construction. Indeed, the fact that the Sorpe was still considered a prime target was hinted at when at 0210 Gibson was asked to confirm if there were any first-wave aircraft left to attack the Sorpe dam (which of course there were not).

Yet that some confusion existed was suggested when at 0221 Bill Townsend in AJ-O was ordered to attack the Ennepe dam by 5 Group. This was at best a minor target and it appeared that breaching it would not make any appreciable difference to the impact of the raids. Nevertheless, it was for the Ennepe reservoir that Townsend now headed. This was odd too given the radio message to Gibson at 0210, which asked him how many aircraft he had left in his wave to attack 'Target C', the Sorpe dam. Gibson had of course replied that he had none but clearly HQ considered the dam an important priority, which does beg the question of why they had not sent all the reserve aircraft there rather than to a purely incidental secondary target like the Ennepe dam.

In any event, at 0224 Ken Brown in AJ-F received the 'Dinghy' message to confirm that the Eder dam had been breached and set off for the Sorpe dam instead of the one at the Eder. It had been a harrowing journey for Brown and his crew so far, having experienced heavy flak over Holland and also witnessing some of their comrades being shot down on their journey to the dams.

As they passed over the town of Hamm, which was known to be well defended, they experienced very heavy fire. The planes were flying so low that the German gunners were actually firing down on them from the lip of a small hill. This was not the only problem for the aircrews either. The high-tension cables en route were a constant menace; a tangle with them would be fatal as other crews had already discovered. Brown's plane had also passed over the Möhne dam, where the gunners whose weapons had not been knocked out in the raid earlier were still quite active.

Down below the Möhne reservoir, the destruction that had been unleashed was still spreading. Further downriver from Neheim, parts of which had been under water since 0120, was Wickede. Hermann Kerstholt was a patient at a military hospital in Arnsberg but had spent the weekend in Wickede, though he had decided to spend Sunday night at Echthausen, closer to the dam. He had a good view over the valley and had been awoken by the sound of low-flying planes. He was later alerted by a rumbling noise and, looking into the distance, saw a 'grey wall' that he quickly realised was a foaming flood rolling down the valley.

As he looked on disbelievingly, he could see, floating on top of the waters, sections of huts with people on them signalling with lights. He could also see from time to time lights flare up and then as quickly be snuffed out, as would happen when a match was being lit. He ran to phone his relatives in nearby Wickede to tell them to get to high ground as quickly as they could. Fortunately, they all survived the inundation.

Hanna Maria Kampschulte was a sixteen-year-old girl in Wickede. She was woken by her mother at 0220 – she had been disturbed by the sound of rushing water and a distant fog even though the moon was bright. The family managed to reach the attic quickly but within minutes the water was up to the level of the top floor. Looking next door, they could see that their neighbour's house had already been washed away.

Soon after, they felt their own floor start to sink. They were forced up against the roof timbers. Hanna managed to push some tiles out and pushed her head through the roof. The next she knew was when the roof was being carried along by the current. Before long, the roof disintegrated around her and she then managed to grab hold of another piece of wreckage which she used as a makeshift raft. She eventually managed to haul herself out of the flood having been carried nearly 10 kilometres away from the site of her home before getting out of the deluge.

But she was still not safe. She hauled herself up into a willow tree, where she found herself in the presence of a cow nearby in the water. The cow was so close that it started to lick her feet. At around 0800 a man waded out to her, up to his shoulders in the water, and at last carried her back to safety. When she went back to her house later that afternoon, it was just a pile of stones and rubble. Tragically, the rest of her family, apart from her father who was away because of the war, were wiped out. Her mother was later buried with her infant son in her arms. Much has rightly been made of the heroism of the raids; less so of the devastation and personal loss that they caused. In war, there is never glory without death.

In the meantime, at 0226 wireless operator George Chalmers (in Townsend's plane AJ-O) reconfirmed a repeat order that had been received to attack the Ennepe dam, the original message not having been responded to – one of several occasions during the raids where communication had not always worked as well as it ideally would. Douglas Webb, the front gunner in the plane, could not speak highly enough of Bill Townsend's flying skills though: according to him they owed their survival to the pilot, who simply got lower and lower in a successful attempt to avoid any problems with flak. 'Bill was the best pilot I ever flew with,' he later said. Despite his best efforts, they still experienced heavy flak on the way in, which Townsend avoided by throwing his 'heavily laden Lancaster around like a Tiger Moth'.

Communications were still coming across the North Sea from England, giving the other pilots in the reserve wave their instructions as far as their targets were concerned. At around 0230 several messages were sent. One was intended for Flight Sergeant Cyril Anderson's plane (AJ-Y). With the Möhne and Eder dams both gone, he was to head for the Sorpe. Pilot Officer Warner Ottley in AJ-C was ordered to target 'Gilbert', the codename for the Lister dam.

But just a couple of minutes later, Ottley too was also ordered to head for the Sorpe, with HQ presumably realising that there were not enough planes headed for it; that it was a hard nut to crack was well known and given its importance it was crucial that as many planes as possible were sent to it. The same message was sent to Burpee in AJ-S but he of course was in no position to respond to it. Belatedly, though, Bomber Command realised that, with the exception of Townsend, focus should be on the Sorpe dam.

In the meantime Gibson's flight was going in the opposite direction, towards England and safety. On the way back, they re-engaged the still active flak positions at the Möhne dam; their instructions were to stick to low-level flying on the return journey as well as on the route out. This of course gave Gibson and his fellow surviving pilots who were with him the chance to inspect their handiwork from earlier on in the night.

As Gibson's plane flew back over the Möhne dam, the impact made through the efforts of 617 Squadron was already very apparent. Pleasure boats lay stranded on the now exposed banks of the dam while bridges peeked up through water like islands in a vast sea that now lapped at the base of the shattered dam. A lake had formed below its broken walls, one that was not stationary but moving clumsily down the valley drowning everything and everyone in its path.

As Edward Johnson looked out from his prime position as bomb-aimer in AJ-N (Les Knight's plane) sand was showing all round the edges of the rapidly emptying lake. The power station in the shadow of the dam wall had disappeared. There were large lumps of masonry scattered around the valley below. All in all it looked a complete mess.

Joe McCarthy had already flown over the Möhne dam and the area below it on the way back from his solo mission to the Sorpe. To him it looked like an inland sea. There was nothing but water visible for miles. McCarthy was experiencing navigational problems on the way back and he had therefore decided to fly back the same way they had come in. They flew by mistake over Hamm but were so low that the guns there were unable to depress their elevation enough to fire at them. McCarthy was lucky to escape from this heavily defended area.

Gibson and his crew passed the Möhne flak positions safely and continued on their homeward journey. As they flew on, Trevor-Roper, his rear gunner – who had a few incendiary bombs left – asked if he could drop them out of the aircraft over any village that happened to be in their path. Gibson assented. Trevor-Roper had got through 12,000 rounds of ammunition during the course of the night and this was all the ammunition he had left.

Front gunner Frederick Sutherland, one of Les Knight's crew, unleashed a hail of bullets at the cab of a train in a small town but the bullets just bounced off. No doubt tensions were high, especially following the death of 'Hoppy' Hopgood, but these actions contrasted with Gibson's own assertions that they were not out to harm civilians but to wipe out industrial targets – 'no one likes mass slaughter, and we did not like being the authors of it. Besides, it brought us into line with Himmler and his boys,' he said.

However, there is evidence to the contrary in Gibson's uncensored account in his *Enemy Coast Ahead*. Here he quoted the story of a Sergeant Knox, whose mother had been killed in a German raid. Knox wished to fly on a raid over Germany as a way of obtaining revenge; in the uncensored account one of the deputy flight commanders was quoted as saying, 'Don't bother about the target tonight chaps, a stick across the town will do for all, and may we kill as many people as possible to avenge Sergeant Knox's mother.' This version of events was removed from the censored version released to the public while the war was still on.

In fact, there is plenty of evidence that 'Hun hate', as it was euphemistically known, was widespread during the war years. Given a civilian population that had endured either first-hand or vicariously episodes like the London Blitz or the bombing of Coventry, there was understandable resentment in many quarters at the devastation that the Luftwaffe had brought to Britain. Not everyone was of this bent of course, but an article in the *Sunday Express* that asked the question 'why all this bosh about being gentle with the Germans after we have beaten them when ALL THE GERMANS ARE GUILTY' would have found a sympathetic hearing among widespread elements of the population.

On the way back from the dams, night fighters were much more active but they still struggled in vain to locate and intercept the bombers flying at low altitude. At one stage, Gibson's plane was followed by a night fighter but he managed to shake it off as he had the advantage of the light being behind him.

However, the death toll for the night was not yet over as far as the British were concerned. At 0235 Ottley's plane (AJ-C) crashed; again this event was witnessed by AJ-F, Brown's aircraft, for whom these several reminders of the frailty of aircraft over enemy territory must have been very disconcerting. Ottley had climbed to 500 feet to get his bearings, another demonstration of the difficulty of keeping on course when flying at low levels.

Ottley's journey had already been eventful. When crossing the Scheldt, rear gunner Frank Tees had exchanged fire with flak positions from his rear turret. At one stage he had noticed the plane pass a church spire which towered above them. However, Ottley's decision to now climb to see where he was could not have been worse timed; he was picked up by several searchlights and immediately found himself the target of a fierce flak barrage.

Frank Tees would normally have been the front gunner but for this raid had transferred to the rear gunner's exposed billet in the back of the plane, an action that would save his life and would cost the man who was normally rear gunner, Harry Strange, his. When the flak started, Tees had felt the shells strike the plane and saw flames streaming from the inner port engine. He heard Ottley say, 'I'm sorry boys, we've had it.'

Ottley had in fact turned south towards the Sorpe dam too early and straight into the heavy defences to the north of Hamm. When the plane was hit, a fierce fire broke out in the fuel tank. The explosion blew off a wing and the plane went crashing into the ground. The bomb on board blew up on impact at the edge of a wood, creating a large crater.

On what appeared to be nothing short of a miraculous escape, Tees had been thrown out of the rear turret and was found some 4 kilometres away from the crash site. He was badly burned and was taken first of all to a hospital and then, when sufficiently recovered, to a POW camp. He would survive the war and return home, living until 1982. When he died, his ashes were interred alongside the graves of the rest of the crew, all of whom had died in the crash on the night of the raids.

A nearby resident, sixteen-year-old Freidrich Kleiböhmer, had been woken by light flak several hours before Ottley's crash. He was roused again when the flak started up once more and got up to see a low-flying plane with an engine ablaze flashing past. He was then aware that the plane had crashed at the edge of some woods. There was an explosion followed 30 seconds later by a much larger one as the bomb self-destructed. Although he was he reckoned 3 kilometres away at the time, the explosion was so strong that he was blown off his feet.

He had an irresistible urge to go and see the damage for himself. It was much further away than he thought. On the edge of some woods he bumped into a school friend. While they were there, they were approached by a figure coming out of the woods. They spoke to him but he did not reply. It suddenly dawned on them that the man – it was Tees – could not speak German and was obviously a survivor from the crash.

Showing commendable nerve, Kleiböhmer managed to give the impression that he was armed and Tees put his hands up while the young man's friend ran into a house and phoned the police. They moved off and a farmer gave Kleiböhmer a hunting gun in case Tees tried to escape. However, he was in no position to do so as he was injured and Kleiböhmer had to help Tees along.

As they walked along, Kleiböhmer started whistling a song. Tees joined in. The image of the British airman and his German captor singing along to 'We're Going to Hang out the Washing on the Siegfried Line' is one of the more incongruous of that extraordinary night. They eventually reached a farmhouse where they went in and Tees sat down. Only then could the extent of his wounds be seen. His hands were badly burned and his chest was hurting. The farmer came in and berated Tees for the damage the RAF was causing. Tees just sat there, too exhausted to care.

A policeman arrived in a taxi about half an hour later to take possession of the prisoner. He asked him in Low German (similar to English) how many men were in the plane. Tees, understanding well enough, said seven. The policeman then said that four bodies had been found and that therefore there must be two men on the run. Tees was taken off, now violently shaking, while the search was on for the two presumed runaways.

However, there were no other survivors of Ottley's crew. Ottley himself was an experienced pilot. Despite being one of the youngest members of 617 Squadron, Ottley had already completed a full tour of operations with 207 Squadron. Hamm was well defended because of the rail-marshalling yards and the anti-aircraft position there had already been alerted by McCarthy's plane searching out a route home, although McCarthy had managed to get through unscathed.

Ottley's plane came down to the north of the village of Kötterberg near Hamm. Brown had seen the aircraft crash with a large explosion; in his own words 'he immediately blew up. His tanks went first and then his bomb ... the whole valley was just one large orange ball.' As well as witnessing the loss of several planes, Brown had already had an exciting trip, attacking three trains, killing five enemy soldiers and wounding eight others. Brown's plane had also received a number of hits from flak. The crew continued to head for the Sorpe dam, hoping to complete the spectacular successes enjoyed by the squadron that night.

Brown and Basil Feneron, his flight engineer, had divided their responsibilities for looking through the windscreen with Brown taking the port side and Feneron the starboard. They then passed information back to Heal, the navigator, to plot his position. Brown continued to fly at very low heights to avoid sharing the fate of some of his comrades, at one stage following the course of a road behind some trees to do so.

At virtually the same time, Henry Maudslay's plane, AJ-Z, was nearing Emmerich in the Netherlands. It was now on fire. Though the anti-aircraft post there had orders not to open fire in case they hit a night fighter in error, the gunners could clearly see that this was an enemy aircraft as it was so low that the markings could be seen. The guns opened up on the plane which went down in flames at Netterden. There were no survivors.

Again, Maudslay was unlucky. Minor errors in navigation could have fatal consequences. Emmerich contained significant oil facilities and was defended by a ring of flak. Several men from gun positions in the town later reported that Maudslay's plane tried to fly directly over the town but was hit by gunfire. There were twelve guns trained on the plane, firing so low that they shot off the tops of nearby poplar trees as they tried to bring the aircraft down.

The other survivors from the first two waves ploughed on determinedly towards England. Just before 0300, Gibson and those with him were in sight of safety. Before them, just a few miles off now, was the North Sea and then the homeward run to Scampton. Gibson flew over first, catching the flak gunners off-guard and roaring overhead and on across the sea, with Shannon not far behind.

Then Gibson and Shannon approached the coast, they had adopted classic rapid escape techniques. They had climbed to 800 feet and then put their planes into a steep dive; this gave them the maximum possible speed to optimise their chances of avoiding flak on the coast. Gibson flew out over the golden sand dunes, lightly lit in pastel shades with the approaching onset of morning. The plane whistled over anti-tank ditches and beach obstacles and on towards safety.

However, 'Dinghy' Young, close behind, was not so fortunate. At 0258 he had been heading for a gap in defences but was possibly flying too high. He was following close behind Gibson and was unlucky as the gunners were now alerted. As he climbed to gain speed, he was perfectly silhouetted against the lightening sky. Young tried to veer away to the north but he was unable to do so.

The flak gunners homed in on him and opened up. The shells struck home and Young lost control. His plane plummeted downwards and crash-landed on a sandbar about 100 yards offshore. The plane broke up on impact and everybody on it was killed. The wreckage remained on the sandbar until 1953 when a fierce storm broke it up. The gunners at Castricum-aan-Zee to the north of Ijmuiden reported shooting down an aircraft they believed to be a Halifax but this was probably Young's Lancaster.

The body of Charles Roberts, Young's navigator, was washed ashore and recovered on 17 May. Several others were recovered during the next two weeks. Having survived both the raid on the Möhne and then that on the Eder, Young was particularly unlucky. It was both poignant and sadly ironic that he had earned his nickname through his skill in surviving crashes at sea. This time, he had simply been too low to do anything about the loss of control when his plane was hit. One of the losses was particularly poignant. Sergeant Nichols, Young's wireless operator, was born on 17 May 1910 and therefore died on his birthday.

There were suggestions later that Young had been flying too high before this. After the raid Maltby and Shannon remarked that they had used Aldis signal lamps to warn him that he was flying at too high an altitude. There were perhaps reasons to wonder whether or not he was a bit ring-rusty; he was not used to Lancasters, had not flown operationally for a time and was accompanied by an inexperienced crew, all factors that might have made him overcautious about flying too low. Whether or not these factors had played on his mind will never be known. He was unlucky; others had better fortune, like Les Knight, who at 0259 also flew to safety over the Dutch coast.

Behind the aircraft, parts of Germany were waking up to scenes of utter chaos. As the day was starting to lighten over Wickede, some miles beneath the Möhne dam, Clemens Mols reassured his wife that the water levels outside were starting to recede. They made their way gingerly down the stairs. On the ground floor there was a deposit of mud about 40 centimetres deep. They struggled to get the ground floor door open but could not do so without the help of others outside as the water had jammed it in. Outside the water was still a metre deep and it would be hours before it receded completely.

There was devastation all around. A metre-deep layer of the railway embankment was gone while a railway engine had been carried away. Two big factories had gone, along with a number of houses. The latter was a dramatic illustration of the human cost of war; not just the balance sheet of war production was affected by the raids.

The residents of the two valleys struggled to come to terms with the immensity of the catastrophe they had experienced. It was hard to take it all in and the damage had not ended yet – the floods did not reach Fröndenburg, further downstream, until 0245. Many bodies were later recovered here, more than 160 of them, having been washed downstream and 26 of them, victims who were never identified, were buried in the town.

But those living below the Eder dam had on the whole fared much better than those beneath the Möhne reservoir. In part this was because the Eder valley was more sparsely populated, but also because there had been a surprisingly effective informal early-warning system that had sprung into action whereby news of the imminent flood had been phoned ahead more effectively; this contrasted with the ineffective arrangements in place in the Möhne valley. But even then it had been awful; the flood levels recorded in the Eder valley, which had been prone to flooding before the dam had been built, were nine times higher than anything seen previously.

In the aftermath of the raids, reasons for the lack of effective early warnings were sought. District President Lothar Eickhoff from one of the main local towns in the area below the dams, Arnsberg, wrote a report and, although one must recognise that he would have good reasons to try and exonerate himself by putting the best spin on things, there is an element of credibility in what he said. He claimed that an early-warning system had been in place by which the watchman at the dams would telephone a warning to Soest to the immediate north of the Möhne dam. From here, the message could be passed on to other towns in the region to warn them.

The fatal flaw was that when the plans were drawn up no one could envisage how devastating the bombs delivered by the British would be. Instead of an envisaged leak of 625 cubic metres per second (based on a breach near the top of the dam) the actual rate was 8,800 cubic metres per second and the speed of the waters released simply overwhelmed the communications network. Yet however convincing this might seem, it of course assumed that a warning would only be given after the breach. If one had been delivered before the fatal moment, when an attack was under way but had not yet been successful, many lives might have been saved. But that would assume the German authorities thinking the unthinkable and accepting that the dams might be breached and moving those in the path of any inundation away from air-raid shelters and up onto higher ground.

Scenes of devastation lay all around. Later that day, another Wickede resident, Max von Booselager, went on a recce trip on his bike. He saw frightened cattle on the embankment and in the woods. In fact, the bellowing of the cattle, which according to some evidenced a certain sixth sense, had alerted a number of residents in the night to the imminent deluge and some owed their lives to them. In Vosswinkel, the first warning had come from a herd of horses stampeding through the town just before the water arrived.

Now a once verdant valley was a wasteland. Meadows and pastures had been washed away or were covered with rubble or sand. The carcasses of animals – cows, sheep, chickens, horses and other animals – were strewn around everywhere. Most people in Wickede had been asleep in their beds when the floods hit and many had died. Perhaps the most poignant and macabre memorial was a child's arm that von Booselager saw sticking up through the mud.

It was ironic that the effect on agriculture had not been considered in the planning for the raids by British strategists, but the impact locally was in fact very significant. The effects of this would be longer term than those of the floods on local industry, which would soon recover. Lost animals could not easily be replaced and lost crops would not return until the following year.

In time though, even the effects on agriculture could be coped with. Crops could be re-sown and the land restored to fertility once more. Animals could be replaced, though with difficulty in the wartime economy. The impact on human beings and their lives, however, could not be so easily dealt with. For some of the inhabitants of the towns and villages affected by the deluge, the effects of these terrible events would last for a lifetime, played out in tortured dreams and tragic remembrances of loved ones who had not survived the fateful night when the dams were burst.

9

Final Attack at the Sorpe: The Last Manoeuvres at Target Z

03.01 – 04.00, Monday 17 May

By 0300 the flood had reached the town of Fröndenburg and was starting to move beyond it. In the town, the waters were so fast flowing that a girder bridge there was washed away. But thoughts of the damage they had caused were far from the minds of the returning British aircrews now. For those who had not yet reached the relative safety of the North Sea, time was running short. Day was now breaking and this disadvantaged the British in two ways. First of all and most obviously, it made the planes much easier targets for both German flak gunners and fighter pilots. But there was also another problem. In the early morning mist, visibility lower down was extremely poor in some places and this would make it much harder for the bombers to identify their targets.

Cyril Anderson had been flying around for some time trying to spot the Sorpe dam without success. At 0310, he gave up and made the decision to turn back after being unable to find it. In addition to his problems in sighting the dam, he was also limited in his ability to fight off any attackers as the rear turret guns of his plane were not working. He had had an uncomfortable approach to the dam. Over Dulmen he had been picked out by searchlights and jamming in the rear turret gun had limited his ability to respond to the defences. He now felt that he was left with no option but to put the safety of his crew first and head back to Scampton. Just as Les Munro had done, he was going against the letter of Gibson's literal orders not to return with a bomb still attached. However, the reaction to his return was rather different. On his return, Gibson was not happy with his performance and he was soon moved to another unit, although he was transferred back to 49 Squadron, eventually dying in a raid over Mannheim.

Back at Scampton, confirmation of the details of the raid was about to be delivered in the best possible way, via the first-hand accounts of a pilot and his crew returning from the raid. At 0311 David Maltby's aircraft (Aircraft AJ-J) successfully touched down at Scampton, the first successful raider to do so. Others were well on the way but despite the existence of three prescribed routes for the return journey, no one really followed them.

For many people back at Scampton there was little sleep that night while they waited for news of what had happened on the raids. Tension was high. There was an intense awareness that something special had been happening overnight even though for all but a select few details were still scarce. Sergeant Jim Heveron later recalled that when they heard that the planes were back in British airspace, they went out to dispersal to count them back in. For the next hour or so they would keep their eyes peeled on the lightening horizon, touched by the rays of the early morning sun, until it was obvious that no one else was coming back.

Another of those there was Ruth Ive, who left her Nissen hut at the crack of dawn to see what was going on. She noticed, as she could not fail to, that there was a number of fire engines and ambulances around – this had clearly been a big raid and no one knew what condition the planes would be in when they made it back. As planes started to arrive, Ruth could see that many of them were in a terrible mess.

But there were still a few pilots flying above the heart of the lion's den and for them a successful homecoming was still a long way off. At around 0300 Ken Brown began his attack at the Sorpe. The valley was now in swirling mist, confirming the visibility problems that

Cyril Anderson had experienced. Like Joe McCarthy, Brown would find it very difficult indeed to position his plane correctly for the bomb-drop.

The approach to the dam was extremely challenging. They had to fly in over the village of Langscheid directly above the target at a height of around 1,000 feet above sea level. From here they had to descend rapidly towards the dam. They then had to reach the optimum height of 60 feet above the target (unlike McCarthy, who had to do this visually, they did at least have the lights to help them). When they had reached this height, the flight engineer (in Brown's case, Basil Feneron) had to adjust the throttle to the lowest practical speed, ideally 180 mph.

To compound their difficulties, on the far side of the dam there was a large hill, unimaginatively known as Hill 321, which they had to climb over rapidly. This required that as soon as the bomb was dropped maximum power was called for, which would – hopefully – enable the plane to pull up sharply and to safety. Once the run had been completed, either successfully or not, the plane would circle back to a point above Langscheid, either to see the results if the bomb had been dropped or to have another go if not.

To make a successful drop required significant skill. If a pilot and his engineer left the escape manoeuvre just a fraction too long then the outcome might be catastrophic. Brown could see the church tower protruding through the fog, which gave him some kind of marker to get his bearings on. However, although he adopted McCarthy's tactics and tried to line up his attack using the church tower initially, it did not work. He came in for his first run but overshot the optimum release point. He had to climb hundreds of feet as quickly as he could in a successful attempt to find a safe escape route. 'It didn't do my nerves any good at all,' he later recalled.

Several accounts of Brown's attack on the Sorpe dam state that he did not adopt the same approach as McCarthy but instead flew down the lake. However, this contradicts the account of Dudley Heal, his navigator. He stated that 'the only way we could attack the Sorpe was to fly as near the dam as possible, at the prescribed height, and fly along the dam instead of at right angles to it as with the others, hoping that the nearer we could get to the dam and the nearer to the centre of it the better'. The bomb would not be spun though as it needed to sink quickly into the water when it dropped.

Brown's first designated target had been the Möhne dam but, with that gone, it was always the intention that he should divert to the Sorpe. Heal stated quite categorically that 'we knew if we had to go to the Sorpe Dam, we'd have to adopt a different technique'. Arguing that Brown attacked the dam from across the lake also makes little sense given Brown's approach; the position of the church on the hill at Langscheid is only useful as a marker when approaching the dam wall from the side, yet Brown categorically stated that he used its spire to line up his attack.

In any event, the definitive version comes from Brown's own official account. All the returning pilots were required to respond to a questionnaire on their return to Scampton. One of the questions was whether their weapon bounced on being dropped and how many times. Brown's answer to this was 'N/A (line bombed)', confirming that he was following the approach of attacking along the dam, as McCarthy had earlier, rather than across the reservoir at right angles to it.

The first attempt to get in the right position for an attack failed. A number of similarly unsuccessful attempts to approach the wall followed. Dudley Heal, Brown's navigator, thought there were six while Sergeant Stefan Oancia thought that there were between six and eight. Becoming increasingly frustrated, and presumably nervous too now that the morning was getting brighter, Brown decided to drop incendiaries to help visibility. They were duly dropped and achieved some success in setting light to some trees and providing some form of illumination.

Whether or not it was this that made the difference, Brown now set out on a run that he was happy with. When just past the midpoint of the dam, bomb-aimer Oancia let the bomb go. As it was not spun it dropped straight down onto the shallow sloping earthen bank and rolled into the water. Seconds after, it erupted with a massive explosion that sent a huge geyser of water into the air. The time was now 0314.

The crew of AJ-F looked on hopefully as the enormous explosion reverberated through the hills but, although the damage was greater than that seen before (which had been caused by McCarthy's attack), the dam was clearly not breached. A 'Goner 78C' message was transmitted from Sorpe ('exploded in contact with the dam, no apparent breach'). The crew could, however, see a crumbling along some 300 feet of the dam.

This last attack was also witnessed by Josef Kesting, who was back inside the power station just at the foot of the air side of the earthen wall. He did not see the plane until it was over the middle of the reservoir – unlike McCarthy, who did not have them fitted, this plane, Kesting noticed, had spotlights shining out from underneath. There was another large explosion and all the windows in the power station were blown out. However, for the time being the turbines carried on working. Stones from the parapet were blown across into the compensating basin behind the dam.

Another witness, Josef Brinkschulte, also saw both explosions. In his view this second one was much larger. The tiles were blown off the roofs of the houses about 500 metres below the dam. All the windows in the immediate area were shattered and all the telephones were cut off.

Post-attack analysis by the Germans showed that the two bombs dropped at the Sorpe fell within 100 feet of each other but exploded just 10 feet below the surface. In actuality, about 230 feet of the crown had crumbled but there were no visible signs of cracks. At the pre-raid briefing Wallis had said that six hits might be needed to break open the dam; only two bombs had been dropped on it.

This was the Germans' one stroke of luck during the night of the raids. The Sorpe dam was positioned at a height of about 1,000 feet above sea level. If the wall had been breached – and given the construction of the dam this would probably have been a slow, drawn-out process rather than the relatively instantaneous explosion seen at the Möhne and Eder dams – then the water would have cascaded down the steep air side into the compensating basin below.

The power station at the foot of the dam would have been overwhelmed at once. The water would then have poured down another relatively confined valley, demolishing several small towns and factories along the way. It would finally have flowed out and added to the deluge created by the breaching of the Möhne dam, uniting with the already devastating flood formed by its destruction to create a massive swollen river that would then have obliterated everything in its path. Towns like Neheim (near where the released waters from the Möhne and Sorpe reservoirs would unite) and others further downstream would then have had an even bigger problem to cope with. But that outcome, at least, was avoided.

There is often overlooked evidence that, in the build-up to the raid on the Sorpe, Wallis was becoming increasingly nervous about the ability of his weapon to breach an earthen dam like this one. He had written in a memo to Bomber Command that it might be necessary to crater the dam on the 'air side' (i.e. the opposite side to that by the reservoir, the 'water side') before attacking it from the water. This might help to weaken it. In the event no such attack was launched and the solid earth banks that protected the concrete core of the dam, while crumbled, stood firm enough to prevent a collapse from occurring.

A reconnaissance flight over the Sorpe dam three days later reported that 'no vital change can be seen except for violent activity on some sort of repair work and clearance of the road over the crest of the dam'. The Sorpe dam had held firm against all that had been thrown against it.

Now, having done what they could, Brown and his crew set their course for home. They would fly back over the nearby Möhne dam and see two breaches, confirmation that there had been happy hunting for at last one group of pilots that night: navigator Heal and bomb-aimer Oancia also thought they saw a third breach on the north-east end of the barrier.

More planes were now starting to arrive back at Scampton. At 0319 Mick Martin and his crew landed safely. Then 4 minutes later it was Joe McCarthy's turn to bring his plane in. Because of his faulty compass equipment, he had successfully retraced his route out back to base. McCarthy had a rough landing due to his damaged starboard tyre. The right wing was very low as a result and struck the ground as they came in. When they finally came to a halt and inspected the aircraft there was also shrapnel damage underneath the navigator's feet which could have been very much worse for him if it had only been a few inches further over. Then it was in for a cup of tea.

The raids were now almost over. There was just one plane left still looking for a target. Bill Townsend was having trouble locating his target and at 0330 was still orbiting around looking for it. His objective was one of the secondary targets, the smaller Ennepe dam. As Townsend had flown in, the floodwaters from the Möhne attack could clearly be seen. In places, only treetops and the roofs of houses could be seen breaking through the floodwaters. Like Brown and his crew, Townsend's team had also seen the disturbing sight of several planes going down on their way in.

As they neared what they thought was the Ennepe dam, they saw a bunch of trees on a hillside looming out of the mist. The bomb-aimer was having difficulty lining up his attack and there was some concern about whether or not they had got the right target. In any event, the spinning action was started and the plane began to shake violently.

There were a number of other dams around the Ennepe so it was hard to be sure that they had found the right one. There was a big lake surrounded by land and trees, being quite hilly in parts in the surrounding countryside. There was little flak to worry about in the area, except for when they flew over a canal while trying to find the right approach.

With the thick mist it had been very hard to find the dam. Then they spotted it, identifying it by a distinctive hill in the vicinity. Townsend made three runs before he was satisfied that he should drop his bomb. On the last of them, the bomb was released. It bounced twice before exploding, creating a spectacular wall of water, about 30 seconds after release but well short of the dam. It was now 0337 and the last bomb of the dam raids had been dropped.

More recent research has suggested why the bomb may have bounced short. Quite simply, according to some historians, it appears that Townsend had attacked the wrong dam, another hint that the pre-raid briefing had not been all that it might have been as far as the reserve wave was concerned. According to these historians, instead of the Ennepe, it was the nearby Bever dam that Townsend attacked. The Bever dam was completely different than the Ennepe, with an almost completely opposite dam-to-reservoir orientation and being an earth rather than gravity dam, the same type as the Sorpe, which had proved so stubbornly obstinate.

It has even been suggested that both dams were attacked that night. There were nuisance raids by Mosquitos over Dusseldorf only some 35 kilometres away from the Bever dam and one suggestion is that one of these dropped a bomb at the Bever. Paul Kaiser was a watchman at the dam and saw a plane attacking the dam there. He was convinced that it was a two-engined plane, which would mean that it could be a Mosquito but not a Lancaster.

Kaiser claimed to be quite knowledgeable about aircraft, which would add credence to his view that this was a Mosquito. But he also noticed that the plane was flying at a low level and it came over three times before it dropped its bomb, which does accord closely (though not completely) with Townsend's own account. And it does seem remarkable that an unidentified 'Mosquito' should be attacking a dam on exactly the same night that the other dams were hit by Lancasters

– especially when no Mosquito had been briefed to attack a dam but, judging by its actions as reported by Kaiser, was taking great pains to ensure that it did so. This evidence points strongly towards the Bever being attacked in error by Townsend.

Yet there is still an element of doubt as Kaiser asserted that the bomb was dropped a distant 800 metres from the dam wall (it did not bounce and exploded where it fell) while Townsend's crew claimed that their bomb exploded 150 feet from the dam wall – a vastly different distance. Kaiser described the explosion as if the bomb just went 'phut' in the water. George Chalmers, Townsend's wireless operator, described a 'quite spectacular … wall of water' after the explosion while Kaiser described it as being 'no higher than the trees on the bank – it was like the way that fizz goes up when you open a bottle of sparkling wine'.

Kaiser also claimed that he could see no lights on the plane (it was, he remarked, a very clear night) while Lance Howard, Townsend's navigator, made a specific mention of how he had great difficulty because of the shaking 6-ton bomb in managing to line the plane up with the two lights.

Most likely the explanation for these contradictions is nothing more than the confusion that sometimes attends witnesses to great events when two witnesses looking at the same scene can actually experience what sound like two very different events. Trauma, fear, the confusion of witnessing something out of the ordinary – all help make bad witnesses out of well-meaning people. Interestingly, there were certainly contradictions between the accounts of crew members who were debriefed on the very morning after the raid.

That there are irreconcilable differences between these two accounts must be accepted, but the most probable explanation for events that night, short of finding a witness at ground level at the Ennepe dam who saw a bomb being dropped, was that Townsend had mistakenly attacked the Bever dam.

That there was a bomb dropped at the Bever that night seems clear enough (unlike the Ennepe dam, where only one bomb was recorded as being dropped during the entire war and that was on the other side of the dam and not on the water). The next morning Kaiser and his wife went down to the reservoir by the Bever dam and raked out red bream and perch that had been killed by a bomb blast. Other locals soon joined them, happy to take advantage of a free top-up to their limited rations.

Kaiser pickled a number of the fish that he had picked up and took them with his troops (he had been home on leave when he witnessed the attacks) on a leave train to Wilhelmshaven. His companions were drinking French cognac and Russian vodka and were soon very drunk. They helped themselves freely to the fish that had been so effectively but unwittingly supplied by the RAF.

For the British, this was a disappointing anti-climax after the spectacular results of earlier in the night. But it was after all only a minor target and the major one, the dam at the Möhne, had been breached, so there was plenty to be pleased about as far as the results of the raid were concerned. But the time for post-raid analysis would have to wait as far as Bill Townsend was concerned. Now his job was to fly his crew safely back across enemy territory at the conclusion of one of the most extraordinary air raids in history.

Daybreak was now not far off. Karl Schütte was still on duty on the Möhne and noted that, as it got light between 0300 and 0400, another aircraft flew over. He later related how 'the last serviceable gun on the approach road fired at it but in vain. This Lancaster shot up a barn in Günne with its machine guns and set it on fire. Our guns below the dam could only engage the aircraft while they were flying away from us otherwise they might have hit us on our towers.' Schütte's active involvement in these extraordinary events was over. For the British raiders who had survived, a safe end to this incredible night was in sight. But for the German civilians in the path of the floods, the horrors were still unfolding.